麦格希 中英双语阅读文库

百科百问

第2辑

【美】布鲁卡 (Milada Broukal) ●主编

胡亚红●译

麦格希中英双语阅读文库编委会●编

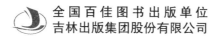

全国百佳图书出版单位
吉林出版集团股份有限公司

图书在版编目（CIP）数据

百科百问. 第2辑 /（美）布鲁卡（Milada Broukal）主编；美国麦格希中英双语阅读文库编委会编；胡亚红译. -- 2版. -- 长春：吉林出版集团股份有限公司，2018.3（2022.1重印）
（麦格希中英双语阅读文库）
ISBN 978-7-5581-4734-0

Ⅰ.①百… Ⅱ.①布… ②美… ③胡… Ⅲ.①英语—汉语—对照读物②科学知识—青少年读物 Ⅳ.①H319.4：Z

中国版本图书馆CIP数据核字(2018)第045915号

百科百问　第2辑

　　　　编：麦格希中英双语阅读文库编委会
插　　画：齐　航　李延霞
责任编辑：朱　玲
封面设计：冯冯翼
开　　本：660mm×960mm　1/16
字　　数：237千字
印　　张：10.5
版　　次：2018年3月第2版
印　　次：2022年1月第2次印刷

出　　版：吉林出版集团股份有限公司
发　　行：吉林出版集团外语教育有限公司
地　　址：长春市福祉大路5788号龙腾国际大厦B座7层
　　　　　邮编：130011
电　　话：总编办：0431-81629929
　　　　　发行部：0431-81629927　0431-81629921(Fax)
印　　刷：北京一鑫印务有限责任公司

ISBN 978-7-5581-4734-0　　　定价：38.00元

前言 *PREFACE*

英国思想家培根说过：阅读使人深刻。阅读的真正目的是获取信息，开拓视野和陶冶情操。从语言学习的角度来说，学习语言若没有大量阅读就如隔靴搔痒，因为阅读中的语言是最丰富、最灵活、最具表现力、最符合生活情景的，同时读物中的情节、故事引人入胜，进而能充分调动读者的阅读兴趣，培养读者的文学修养，至此，语言的学习水到渠成。

"麦格希中英双语阅读文库"在世界范围内选材，涉及科普、社会文化、文学名著、传奇故事、成长励志等多个系列，充分满足英语学习者课外阅读之所需，在阅读中学习英语、提高能力。

◎难度适中

本套图书充分照顾读者的英语学习阶段和水平，从读者的阅读兴趣出发，以难易适中的英语语言为立足点，选材精心、编排合理。

◎精品荟萃

本套图书注重经典阅读与实用阅读并举。既包含国内外脍炙人口、耳熟能详的美文，又包含科普、人文、故事、励志类等多学科的精彩文章。

◎功能实用

本套图书充分体现了双语阅读的功能和优势，充分考虑到读者课外阅读的方便，超出核心词表的词汇均出现在使其意义明显的语境之中，并标注释义。

鉴于编者水平有限，凡不周之处，谬误之处，皆欢迎批评教正。

我们真心地希望本套图书承载的文化知识和英语阅读的策略对提高读者的英语著作欣赏水平和英语运用能力有所裨益。

丛书编委会

Contents

Why Is Louis Pasteur Important?

ouis Pasteur was one of the first people to discover that *diseases* come from *germs*. The word pasteurize that we usually see on milk containers comes from his name.

Louis Pasteur was born in 1822 in a small village in France. As a boy, Louis was interested in art and was a very good

---

为什么巴斯德·路易斯很重要？

巴斯德·路易斯是第一批发现疾病来自细菌的人之一。我们经常在牛奶包装上看到的"巴氏灭菌法"就来源于他的名字。

巴斯德·路易斯于1822年出生在法国的一个小山村。尽管是一个男孩，巴斯德·路易斯却对艺术很感兴趣，他还能画一手好画。但他的父亲并不希

---

disease *n.* 疾病

germ *n.* 细菌

1

painter. His father did not want his son to be an artist when he grew up. He wanted Louis to be a great teacher. Louis was also interested in *chemistry* and other sciences, so he agreed with his father and decided to go to college.

After college, Louis attended a famous school in Paris that trains teachers, the École Normale Supérieure. He entered the school in 1843 to study how to teach chemistry and physics. He soon made a name for himself with his research. After he graduated, he became a professor at the University of Strasbourg. At the university, he met Marie Laurent, the daughter of the director of the university. They fell in love and married in 1849. They were very happy and had five children. Sadly, only one boy and one girl lived to be adults.

In 1854, Louis took a job at the University of Lille, a city in the north of France. He was a professor of chemistry and *dean* of the

---

望儿子长大后成为一个艺术家，而是想让他变成著名的教师。巴斯德·路易斯对化学及其他学科也很感兴趣，因此他顺从父亲的意愿决定去读大学。

大学毕业后，巴斯德·路易斯上了巴黎一所著名的师范学校——巴黎高等师范学院。他1843年入学，开始学习如何讲授化学和物理，很快便因自己的研究而闻名。毕业后，他成为斯特莱斯博格大学的一名教授。在学校时他与校长的女儿玛丽劳伦特相识，相爱，并于1849年结婚，生活得非常幸福。他们共有5个孩子，但不幸的是只有一个男孩和一个女孩活了下来。

1854年，巴斯德·路易斯在法国北部的里尔大学开始新的工作。他是一位化学教授，还是科学系的主任——对于一个年仅32岁的人来说这是

---

chemistry *n.* 化学

dean *n.* 系主任

faculty of science—a very high position for a man of thirty-two. Around this time, the French wine industry was in terrible trouble. Their wine was *sour* and they didn't know why. The winemakers around Lille asked Pasteur to help them. After many experiments, Louis discovered that the problem came from germs. The solution was to heat the wine. This would kill the *harmful* germs. The winemakers were shocked, but the method worked. Soon they also heated other drinks such as beer and milk. This made them safe to drink. The method was called pasteurization, after Louis Pasteur.

In 1857, Pasteur returned to Paris to become director of science studies at the École Normale Supérieure. At that time, there was a terrible disease called anthrax. It killed thousands of sheep and cows every year. Pasteur noticed something interesting. If an animal was

---

相当高的职位了。此时，法国的酒业陷入了严重的危机，酒开始变酸，人们却不知道其中的原因。里尔大学附近的造酒商请求巴斯德·路易斯帮助他们，经过多次实验后，巴斯德·路易斯发现问题来自于细菌。解决的方法就是把酒加热，这样就能杀死有害的细菌。酒商们虽然很震惊，但这方法确实奏效，很快他们开始加热啤酒和牛奶，使它们能够安全地饮用。这种方法后来被称作巴氏灭菌法，名字来自于巴斯德·路易斯。

1857年，巴斯德·路易斯回到了巴黎，担任巴黎高等师范学院的科研系主任。此时，一种名为天花的可怕疾病出现了，这种疾病每年都要夺走数以千计牛羊的生命。巴斯德·路易斯注意到一个有趣的现象，在牲畜感染过一次天花并痊愈后，它终身都不会再患上这种疾病。于是他决定为

---

sour *adj.* 酸的；发酵的   harmful *adj.* 有害的；伤害的

sick with anthrax and got well, it never caught the disease again. He decided to *inject* healthy sheep with weak anthrax germs. These sheep lived and never caught the disease. Pasteur had a *vaccine* against anthrax!

One day in 1885, a doctor brought a nine-year-old boy named Joseph Meister to Pasteur. A mad dog with the disease *rabies* bit the boy, and the doctor didn't know how to save him. In the past, Pasteur helped animals with this disease, but would his method work on humans, or would the boy die? Pasteur was very worried, but finally he tried an experiment. He injected Joseph with his vaccine and sat by his bed to watch the result. The boy lived! Immediately the news spread around the world, and Pasteur was famous.

Pasteur wanted to build a research institute in Paris to continue

---

健康的绵羊注射弱化了的天花病毒，这些绵羊存活了下来并且再也没得这种病，巴斯德·路易斯发现了一种能够对付天花的疫苗！

1885年的一天，一位医生带了个名叫约瑟夫·梅斯特的9岁男孩来见巴斯德·路易斯。他被一条患有狂犬病的狗咬伤了，医生不知道怎么救治他。过去，巴斯德·路易斯救治过患这种疾病的动物，但这种方法适用于人吗，或者说，男孩能被救活吗？巴斯德·路易斯非常担心，最后他决定做一个实验。他给约瑟夫注射了疫苗，坐在他的床边观察效果。男孩活了下来！消息立刻传遍整个世界，巴斯德·路易斯一举成名。

巴斯德·路易斯想在巴黎建一个研究所继续他的工作。世界各地的人

---

inject *v.* 注入；注射　　　　　　　　　　　　vaccine *n.* 疫苗
rabies *n.* 狂犬病

his work. People read about his methods and sent money from all over the world to help build the institute. The Pasteur Institute opened its doors in 1888. It is still one of the world's most respected centers for the study of diseases and how to fight them. Pasteur was the director of the Institute and he worked there until he died in 1895. Everyone remembered Pasteur as a great man.

Years later, during World War II, the Germans came to Paris. A German officer wanted to open Pasteur's *tomb*, but the old French guard said no. When the German *demanded* that he open it or die, the guard killed himself. The name of the guard was Joseph Meister.

们听说后纷纷为他捐款帮助他建立研究所。1888年，巴斯德·路易斯的研究所成立了，现在他的研究所由于在病毒学和治疗领域的研究仍然是世界上最受人尊重的研究中心之一。巴斯德是研究所的领袖人物，他一直在这从事研究工作，直到1895年离世。在所有人心中巴斯德是一个伟大的人。

多年以后，二次世界大战期间，德军占领了巴黎。一名德国的军官想打开巴斯德·路易斯的坟墓，但是年迈的法国卫兵坚决不允许。当德军命令他要么打开坟墓要么选择死亡的时候，卫兵自杀了。这名卫兵就是约瑟夫·梅斯特。

---

tomb *n.* 坟墓   demand *v.* 要求

02

Who Is Nasreddin Hodja?

Everybody in Turkey knows the stories about Nasreddin Hodja. These funny stories are part of Turkish folk culture. Nasreddin Hodja was a man who lived near Ankara, in central Turkey, in the thirteenth century. The *jokes* and stories are about Nasreddin's *daily life*. Some of these stories are

纳斯雷丁·霍加是谁？

在土耳其，每个人都知道纳斯雷丁·霍加的故事，这些有趣的故事已经成为土耳其民间文化的一部分。霍加13世纪生活在土耳其中部的安卡拉附近。这些故事是关于霍加的日常生活的，有些已经有800年的历史了，但仍然有趣。下面就是一些关于霍加的故事。

---

joke *n.* 玩笑；笑话   daily life 日常生活

about eight hundred years old, and they are still funny. Here are some Nasreddin Hodja stories.

The Pot That Gave Birth

Nasreddin Hodja borrowed a large pot from his neighbor. Days and weeks passed, but he didn't return the pot. One day the neighbor came over and asked to have his pot back. Hodja *apologized*, "I am sorry. I forgot to return it." But, he said, "I have good news for you. While the pot was at my house, it *gave birth to* a smaller pot."

Hodja handed his neighbor the big pot and the "baby" pot, and the neighbor went home happily with two pots.

A few weeks later, Hodja knocked on his neighbor's door and asked to borrow the large pot again. The neighbor remembered the good experience from the first time, so he was happy to lend his pot to Hodja again.

会生孩子的锅

霍加从他的邻居那里借了一口大锅，几个星期过去了仍没有还。一天邻居来要锅，霍加抱歉地说，"对不起，我忘了还你了，但我有一个好消息要告诉你，锅在我家的时候生了一口小锅。"

霍加把大锅和婴儿锅一起还给了邻居，邻居拿着两个锅高高兴兴地回家了。

几星期之后，霍加又敲开了邻居的门向他借那口大锅。邻居想起第一次借锅的愉快经历，于是非常高兴地又把锅借给了他。

---

apologize *v.* 道歉　　　　　give birth to 产生；出生

Weeks passed and there was no word from Hodja about the pot. The neighbor decided to go to Hodja's house, as before, and ask him to *return* the pot. When Hodja opened the door, the neighbor asked to have the pot back. Hodja, with a sad face, told the man that the large pot died.

The neighbor was shocked and angry and said,"What do you think I am, an *idiot*? Do you want me to believe that a pot died?"

"My good man," Hodja replied with a smile,"you had no trouble believing that a pot gave birth."

Tiger Powder

One day Nasreddin Hodja was outside. His neighbor saw Hodja putting some powder on the ground around his house. The neighbor

---

几个星期过去了，霍加还没有把锅还回来。邻居决定像以前一样去他家让他还锅，霍加开门后，邻居让他还锅。霍加哭丧着脸告诉他大锅死了。

邻居非常震惊和生气地说："你把我当成了什么，一个傻瓜吗？你让我相信一个锅会死吗？"

"我的好邻居"，霍加微笑着说，"可是对锅会生孩子你却一点也不怀疑啊。"

驱虎粉

一天，霍加正在外边干活。邻居看见霍加在房子周围的地面上撒了许

---

return *v.* 归还   idiot *n.* 笨蛋；傻瓜

asked, "Hodja, what are you doing?"

Hodja replied, "I want to keep the tigers away."

The neighbor said, "But there are no tigers within hundreds of miles."

"*Effective*, isn't it?" Hodja replied.

The *Opinions* of Men

Hodja and his son went on a journey to another town. They only had one donkey. Hodja told his son to ride the donkey. Hodja preferred to walk. On the way, they met some people who said, "Look at that healthy boy! That's today's youth. They have no respect for their elders. He is riding on the donkey and his poor

---

多粉末。邻居问，"霍加，你在干什么？"

霍加答道，"我想把老虎赶走。"

邻居说，"但是方圆百里内并没有老虎啊。"

"这不正说明我的方法很有效吗？"霍加回答。

别人的看法

霍加和他的儿子出发去另一个城镇，但他们只有一头驴。霍加让儿子骑驴，因为他自己更喜欢走路。路上，有的人说，"看看那个身强力壮的孩子！这就是现在的年轻人，他们根本不知道尊重长辈。自己骑着驴却让

---

effective *adj.* 有效的   opinion *n.* 意见

father is walking!"

When they passed these people, the boy felt bad. He told his father to ride the donkey while he walked. So Hodja rode the donkey, and the boy walked at his side.

A little later, they met other people who said,"Well, look at that! That poor boy has to walk while his father is riding the donkey."

After they passed these people, Hodja told his son, "The best thing is for both of us to walk. Then, no one can *complain*." So they continued their journey on foot, walking beside the donkey.

Down the road, they met some others who said, "Just look at those idiots. Both of them are walking under this hot sun and neither of them is riding the donkey!"

Hodja turned to his son and said, "That shows you how hard it is to *escape* the opinions of men."

老父亲走路！"

男孩听后很羞愧，于是他让父亲骑驴自己走路。于是霍加骑上了驴，男孩在旁边跟着走。

过了一会，他们又碰到一群人说，"看哪！那个可怜的孩子只能走路，他爸爸却骑着驴。"

等这些人走过后，霍加告诉儿子，"我们俩最好的方式就是都走路，这样就没人抱怨了。"于是他们继续走路，走在毛驴的旁边。

过了一会，又听见有人说，"看那两个傻瓜，两个人都在太阳下走路，有驴却不知道骑。"

霍加转过头来对儿子说，"现在知道想避开别人的议论是多么困难了吧。"

---

complain *v.* 抱怨　　　　　　　　　　　　　escape *v.* 避开；避免

Backward Donkey

One day, Nasreddin Hodja got on his donkey the wrong way, facing backward.

"Hodja," the people said,"you are sitting on your donkey backward!"

"No," he replied."I am sitting on the donkey *correctly*. It is the donkey that is facing backward."

The stories of Nasreddin Hodja are now in many languages. They are popular all over the world. In honor of Nasreddin Hodja, UNESCO (The United Nations Education, Scientific, and Cultural Organization) decided to call 1996—1997 International Nasreddin Hodja Year.

向后走的驴

一天，霍加骑驴时坐反方向，脸朝后面了。

"霍加，"别人告诉他说，"你骑驴的方向搞反了。"

"没有，"霍加答道，"我骑驴的方向是对的，是驴把方向搞错了。"

霍加的故事现在被译成了很多种语言，全世界都很流行。为纪念霍加，联合国教科文组织决定把1996年-1997年命名为国际霍加年。

---

correctly *adv.* 正确地

What Did the Ancient Mayans Believe In?

The Mayan people of Mexico and Central America had the greatest *civilization* in the New World. The height of Mayan civilization was between 250 and 900. At this time, there were about fourteen million Maya. In forty of their cities, they built huge *pyramids* that were

古玛雅人信仰什么?

在新大陆的墨西哥和中美洲生活的玛雅人曾经有高度发达的文明。玛雅文明的鼎盛期出现在公元250年到900年。那时,玛雅人的总人口达到了1400万。在他们的40个城市中,他们修建了一些高达22

civilization *n.* 文明;文化   pyramid *n.* 金字塔

twenty-two stories high. Why did they build these pyramids? How did the Maya create their civilization? How did they structure their lives and society? Their beliefs guided them.

The Maya believed in time and numbers. They had a great knowledge of mathematics. They invented a number system that used only three symbols, and they invented zero. What would mathematics be without zero? They also made a calendar 2,600 years ago that was very *accurate*. It had 365 days in a year. There were three kinds of days on their calendar: good, bad, and *neutral*. People did important things on good or neutral days. They went on a journey, got married, or planted corn only on a good day. Time had a beginning and an end, too. They believed the world was going to end in 2012.

层的巨形金字塔。玛雅人为什么要修建这些金字塔？玛雅人是如何创造他们的文明的？他们是如何经营自己的生活和社会的？答案是他们的信仰指引了他们。

玛雅人相信时间和数字。他们对数学有着深入的研究。他们发明了一套只有3个符号的数字系统，还发明了数字0的概念。想象数学里如果没有了0会怎么样？他们还在2600年前就创造出了一套非常精确的历法，历法的每年包括365天，历法上的日子分为三种：好，坏和中等。人们在好和较好的日子做重要的事情，而且只在好的日子外出旅行、结婚或种植玉蜀黍。时间有开始也有结束，他们相信世界会在2012年终结。

---

accurate *adj.* 正确的；精确的

neutral *adj.* 中立的；中性的

The Maya also believed in *astrology*; they believed that you could find all truth in the movement of the stars, the sun, and the moon. Astrology controlled their lives and their culture. The priests *predicted* the future by astrology. They did not have telescopes, but they knew all about the sky. The priests were called "He who knows" and were very important. They wore jewels and special feathers. People carried the priests on their shoulders in the streets. Everyone listened to the priests and believed in their predictions.

As soon as a baby was born, parents took it to the priest. The priest told the parents about the child's *destiny*. Each day on the Mayan calendar says what a baby born on that day will become. Parents had to bring up the child to be a farmer, a poet, a dancer, or another job the priest predicted. Each person lived according to his or her destiny.

　　玛雅人同样相信天象；他们相信真理存在于星星，太阳和月亮的运动中。天象掌控着他们的生活和文化，巫师们通过天象预测未来。他们没有望远镜，但他们对天体很了解。巫师们被称作"无所不知的人"，地位非常重要。他们佩戴珠宝和特殊的羽毛，人们在街道上用肩膀扛着巫师行进。每个人都会听从巫师的话并且相信他们的预言。

　　每个婴儿出生后父母都会把他带到巫师那里，让巫师告知他们婴儿的命运。玛雅历法的每一天都会告知在那一天出生的婴儿的命运。父母们会按照巫师的预言把孩子培养成农民、诗人、舞蹈家或从事其他工作，每个人都会遵从命运生活。

---

astrology *n.* 占星学；占星术　　　　　　　　　　predict *v.* 预知；预言
destiny *n.* 命运

The priests studied the sky to collect information, then they wrote their predictions in books. The Maya invented a writing *system* that used picture symbols. This was the first writing system in the Americas. They used tree bark for paper and made many books. Only a few books survive. We found a few of these books, but nobody could understand the writing. About fifty years ago, a researcher finally uncovered the meaning of the symbols. That is how we know about Mayan beliefs and predictions.

The Maya believed in many gods: the sun god, the moon god, and many other gods from nature. But the corn god was the most important. Without corn, they had no food. They believed all people came from the corn god. When a child was born, they put the head of the baby between two pieces of wood for several days. The shape of the baby's head became *permanently* flat and long. They thought this long, flat head looked like corn, which was a sign of high class.

巫师们通过观察天象以收集信息，然后把预言写进书里。玛雅人发明了一套应用符号语言的书写系统，这是美洲大陆的第一套书写系统。他们用树皮造纸写了很多书，但只有很少的一部分保存了下来。人们找到了一些这样的书，但没人能理解书中文字的含义。50年前，一名研究者终于弄清了这些符号代表的意思，我们便能理解玛雅人的信仰和预言。

玛雅人信仰许多神：太阳神、月亮神以及许多其他自然界的神。但玉蜀黍神是最重要的，因为没有玉蜀黍，他们就没有食物。他们相信所有的人都是玉蜀黍神的后代。孩子出生后，会把婴儿的头放在两片木板间夹上几天，于是婴儿的头从此变得又长又扁。他们认为这种又长又扁的头型看

system *n.* 系统   permanently *adv.* 永久地

They also hung a small ball or bead from the baby's hair so that it fell between the baby's eyes. The child looked at this ball and later became cross-eyed. This was also a sign of beauty and high class.

Around the year 900, the Maya disappeared. We do not know what happened. Later, the Spanish came to their land and *destroyed* what was left of the Mayan culture, including most of the books filled with their predictions. The *descendants* of the Mayan people still exist in Mexico and other countries of Central America, such as El Salvador, Guatemala, and Belize. There are still Mayan priests among them, and they still use the old Mayan calendar to make predictions.

起来很像玉蜀黍，是身份高贵的象征。他们也会在婴儿的头发上拴上小球或小珠让它们垂下来时正好位于婴儿的两眼之间，婴儿看着球，眼睛慢慢就变成了对眼，这也是一种美丽和高贵的象征。

公元900年前后，玛雅文明消失了。人们不知道发生了什么事。后来，西班牙人来到了这里，毁掉了玛雅文明残存的部分，其中包括记载有他们预言的大部分书籍。玛雅人的后代现在仍生活在墨西哥和中美洲的其他一些国家，比如萨尔瓦多、危地马拉和博立兹城。他们中间仍有玛雅巫师，巫师们依然使用玛雅日历进行预言。

---

destroy *v.* 消灭；毁坏   descendant *n.* 子孙；后裔

How Do Koreans Celebrate a Wedding?

In the past, parents in Korea *arranged* marriages for their children. Usually, they hired a *matchmaker* to help them. A matchmaker was usually a woman in the village. People paid her to find a good match for their son or daughter. The couple usually did not meet each other until the day of the wedding.

韩国人如何庆祝婚礼?

过去,韩国人的婚姻都是父母包办的。通常他们会请媒婆帮忙,媒婆一般是村子里的女人。他们给媒婆钱让她为子女寻找一位好伴侣。结婚前夫妻双方一般是不见面的。

arrange *v.* 安排　　　　　　　　matchmaker *n.* 媒人

Today there are two ways to get married in Korea. The first is by a love match: two people meet, fall in love, and get married. There is no need for a third person. The second way is an arranged marriage: a third person chooses two people to marry each other, and if the two families agree, the next step is to visit the *fortune-teller*.

Koreans believe in the "four pillars." These are the year, month, day, and hour of a person's birth. A fortune-teller uses these four things to predict your destiny. Before a couple gets married, the fortune-teller looks at their four pillars to see whether they can be happy together. If the four pillars are bad for the couple, the family returns to the matchmaker to try again. If the four pillars are good for the couple, they can get engaged.

At the engagement *ceremony*, the two families get together. They can meet at the girl's house, a hotel, or a restaurant, but never at

---

今天在韩国有两种结婚的方式。第一种是两情相悦。两个人相识，相爱并最终结合。这种方式不需要第三方的帮助。第二种是包办婚姻，第三方选择两个人结婚，如果双方家庭同意，那么下一步就是去见预言师。

韩国人相信四时，即一个人生日的年、月、日和时。预言师利用这四个方面来预测人的命运。每对新人结婚前，预言师会查看他们的四时以决定他们是否能幸福地生活在一起。如果四时不配，家人就会重回媒婆那里请她重新物色。如果四时合适，二人就可以订婚。

订婚仪式上，两个家庭在一起聚会。他们会选择在女孩的家、宾馆或饭店聚会，但决不在男孩的家中。今天，双方的家人通常在饭店聚会并为

---

fortune-teller 算命者

ceremony *n.* 典礼；仪式

the boy's house. Today, families usually meet in a restaurant to set a date for the wedding. They always give each other lots of gifts. The two young people also exchange gifts. Some Korean families spend $30,000 to $40,000 on engagement gifts. One of the gifts to the girl's family is a special document. In the middle of a piece of expensive paper, her husband's four pillars are written in ink. The girl keeps this document all her life.

The time before the marriage ceremony is very exciting for the boy, called the *groom*, and the girl, called the *bride*. The groom's family sends a box of gifts (called a hahm) for the bride. Usually, the gifts are jewelry and red and blue fabric for a traditional dress. Friends of the groom *deliver* the box at night. They shout playfully, "Buy a hahm! Hahm for sale!" The friends wait for the family to give them food and money, then they give the box of gifts to the girl.

婚礼选定日期。他们互相交换很多礼物，两个年轻人也会互换礼物。一些韩国家庭为订婚仪式要花费30,000到40,000美元。女孩家收到的礼物之一是一份特别的文件，她丈夫的四时写在一张很昂贵的纸上。女孩会终生保存这份文件。

　　对于新娘和新郎来说，婚礼前是非常兴奋的。新郎的家庭要把一盒礼物送给新娘。通常，礼物是珠宝和为传统服装准备的红蓝织物。新郎的朋友们会在夜间把盒子送过去，他们会开玩笑地大声喊，"来买阿兹特克啦，谁买阿兹特克！"这些人会等新娘的家人送给他们食物和钱后再把礼物盒交给女孩。

---

groom *n.* 新郎   bride *n.* 新娘
deliver *v.* 递送；传送

The day of the wedding arrives! Traditionally, the groom first gives his new *mother-in-law* the gift of a goose. The goose is a symbol of love because a goose takes only one partner in its life. Today, the groom gives a goose made of wood. Then it's time for the ceremony. They have the ceremony at a table. The bride and groom sit at the table. They each have a cup full of a special wine, and they take a sip. Then someone takes the cups, mixes together the wine, and pours it into their cups again. The bride and groom each sip the mixed wine. This is a symbol of their new life together.

Korean Americans have a ceremony that is a little different. Family and close friends attend the ceremony. The new wife offers her in-laws gifts of dried fruits that represent children. This is a symbol of her wish to give them grandchildren. Her in-laws offer her tea. At the end of the ceremony, they throw fruit and *chestnuts* at the bride, and

---

　　婚礼的日子到了。按照传统，新郎要送给他的岳母一只鹅。鹅是爱情的象征，因为鹅的一生中只有一个伴侣。现在，新郎们通常会送木鹅。接下来就是婚礼仪式了。新郎新娘在桌边坐好，每人面前有一只斟得满满的酒杯，他们会轻啜一口。然后有人拿起杯子，把酒混合在一起后重新倒入杯中。新郎新娘轮流喝掉混合后的酒，这是他们新生活开始的标志。

　　在韩国生活的美国人的订婚仪式稍有不同。家人和好友会参加仪式，新娘会为新郎的父母献上代表孩子的干果，这表示她愿意为他们生很多的孙子孙女。他们会回赠她茶叶。在仪式结束的时候，人们向新娘抛掷水果和栗子，新娘会用自己的裙子去接住它们。

---

mother-in-law 岳母　　　　　　　　　　　　chestnut *n.* 栗子

she tries to catch them in her skirt.

The wedding *banquet* follows. It is called "the noodle banquet" because there is a lot of noodle soup. As in China, noodles represent a long and happy life. For *dessert*, there are sweet cakes and a sweet, sticky rice ball. It has chestnuts, jujubes, raisins, and pine nuts. These are all symbols of children.

When the eldest son of a family gets married, it is traditional for his parents to move in with him and his new wife. This shows that the son will always take care of his parents, and that his wife will take care of his parents also.

接下来是婚礼酒会，也被称为面条酒会，因为会有许多面条汤。在中国，面条代表一种长久而幸福的生活。至于甜点，通常会有甜蛋糕和一种又甜又粘的饭团，里面有栗子、红枣、葡萄干和松果，这些都是象征着孩子。

当一个家族的长子结婚后，按照传统，他的父母会搬进来与新婚夫妇同住。这表示儿子将一直照顾父母，他的妻子也同样会一起照顾丈夫的父母。

---

banquet *n.* 宴会　　　　　　　　　　dessert *n.* 餐后甜点

Why Are Sumo **W**restlers So Fat?

It is very difficult to stop a train, a ship, or any large object that is moving. The same is true for a *sumo wrestler*. A big wrestler is hard to move. It is easier for him to move you—like a train that hits a bicycle.

Sumo is a kind of wrestling that comes from Japan. It is Japan's national sport. The *origin* of sumo wrestling is religious. It came from Japan's Shinto

---

相扑运动员为什么那么胖?

当一辆火车、轮船或任何大家伙移动起来的时候让它停下是很难的。相扑运动员亦是如此,一个体形庞大的相扑选手是很难撼动的,而他却能轻易地撞开你——就像火车撞自行车一样。

相扑是源于日本的一种摔跤术,是日本的国粹。相扑的起源是带有宗教色彩的,它来自于日本的神道教。你能从这种运动的方方面面看到宗教

---

sumo *n.* 相扑
origin *n.* 起源;由来

wrestler *n.* 摔跤选手

religion. You can see the effect of the religion in every part of the sport. For example, the ring, or *dohyo*, looks like a Shinto temple. The dohyo is fifteen feet across and two feet high. All the *decorations* are Shinto symbols, too.

Each sumo match starts with a traditional ceremony. The ceremony is as important as the wrestling, and the people like to watch it. Each movement in the ceremony has a special meaning. To begin the ceremony, the wrestlers face each other and raise their arms. In the past, this was to show that they didn't have any knives. Then they clap their hands and stamp their feet. In the past, this was to chase away demons, or bad spirits. Each wrestler has a *unique* style for his movements. One wrestler may finish the ceremony in one minute, another may take three minutes. The last part of the ceremony is to throw salt in the ring. This means that the ring is

---

的影响。例如，比赛用的圆形场地直径十五英尺，高两英尺，所有装饰物都标志着神道教，看上去像神道教的庙宇。

每场相扑比赛的开始都有一个传统仪式。仪式和比赛是同样重要的，人们也都很喜欢。仪式中的每个动作都有它特殊的含义。仪式开始时，相扑选手面对面站立并举起前臂，在过去这表示他们没有带任何刀具。然后他们击掌，跺脚，过去这表示驱走魔鬼和恶灵。每个相扑选手都有自己一套独特的动作，有人可能用一分钟完成，有人可能要花三分钟。仪式的最后一项是向场地中撒盐，这表示场地是干净的。

---

dohyo *n.* 相扑赛场   decoration *n.* 装饰
unique *adj.* 独特的；稀罕的

clean and ready to use.

After the ceremony, the wrestling match starts. The basic rules of sumo are simple and few, which means that matches can be very exciting. During the match the wrestler can't pull hair, hit with a closed *fist*, or choke the other wrestler(but he may push at his throat). He can do anything else. The first wrestler who touches the ground with anything except his feet or steps out of the ring is the loser. Five judges watch the match. A match only lasts a few seconds and *rarely* lasts one minute.

To become a sumo wrestler you must first join a stable. To enter a stable, you must be fifteen to twenty-two years old. You must be at least five feet seven inches tall and weigh at least 165 pounds. Parents must agree to let their son join a stable, and he must pass

---

仪式过后，比赛就开始了。相扑比赛的基本规则很少而且很简单，这意味着比赛会很激烈。比赛过程中选手不能互扯头发，用拳击打对方或是令对方窒息（但可以推对方的喉咙），除此以外可以做任何动作。在比赛中除脚之外的身体其他任何部分着地或踏出场地即被判负。五名裁判监督比赛，比赛通常只有几秒钟，持续一分钟的比赛都很少见。

想成为相扑运动员首先要加入一个门派，想加入这个门派，你必须在15岁—22岁之间，至少5英尺7英寸高，165磅重，且必须经过父母的同意才能加入，然后还要通过身体测试。加入门派之后，相扑选手就在那里生活和训练，他一生中的其余时间就都属于这个门派了。

---

fist *n.* 拳头

rarely *adv.* 很少地；难得

a physical exam. When he joins a stable, a wrestler trains and lives there. He is part of that stable for the rest of his life.

In a stable, rank is extremely important. New members start training at 4:30 or 5:00 a.m. In the beginning, new wrestlers do the housework nobody likes. They prepare lunch, clean, wash clothes, and do many other chores. Wrestlers of low rank always *serve* wrestlers of high rank.

Weight is important to sumo wrestlers. When they join a stable, wrestlers may weigh less than 200 pounds, but they must gain weight to advance. The average weight of a top-rank wrestler is 335 pounds. Wrestlers are big, but they are not all fat. They have strong muscles in their arms and legs. They are also very *flexible*. Some sumo wrestlers have less body fat than the average businessman. Weight is important, but they must also have speed, strength,

---

在门派中，级别是极其重要的。新队员们早晨4:30到5:00开始训练。开始的时候，新队员要做那些没人愿做的家务活。他们准备午餐，洗衣服，做很多杂活，级别低的相扑选手要为级别高的服务。

体重对于相扑选手来说很重要。当他们刚加入门派时，相扑选手可能还不到200磅，但他们必须要增加体重才能进步。第一流的相扑选手的体重是335磅。他们体型庞大，但身上并不全是肥肉，他们的胳膊和大腿有强健的肌肉。他们的柔韧性同样非常好，某些相扑运动员的脂肪含量要低于一般的商人。体重很重要，但他们也要有速度、力量、平衡和技巧。相扑运动员

---

serve *v.* 招待；伺候

flexible *adj.* 灵活的

balance, and technique. Sumo wrestlers can have health problems because of their weight, too. They often have heart trouble, high blood pressure, *diabetes*, and injuries from wrestling. Most wrestlers try to lose weight after they retire.

It is not easy for some wrestlers to get big. They don't eat candy or other junk food to gain weight. They eat large portions of high-calorie food with lots of rice. Some wrestlers eat 20,000 *calories* a day. That's ten times the calories an average person eats. They also exercise a lot to build muscle.

In Japan, sumo wrestlers are national heroes. They are as popular as movie stars. The Japanese believe that sumo wrestlers bring good luck. If a sumo wrestler of high rank picks up a baby, the baby will grow big and strong. They are also popular with women. Sumo wrestlers often marry models, actresses, or television stars.

也会因体重的原因带来健康问题。心脏病、高血压、糖尿病是他们中的常见病，以及相扑比赛带来的外伤。大多数相扑选手退役后都要尝试着减肥。

相扑选手想拥有庞大的体型并不容易，他们并不靠吃糖或其他垃圾食品来增重。他们的饮食中高热量的食物比重很大，另外他们还要吃大量的米饭。有些相扑选手每天要摄入20,000卡路里，是一般人的10倍。他们也进行大量的训练用以锻炼肌肉。

在日本，相扑运动员是国家英雄，他们和电影明星一样受到大众的欢迎。人们认为相扑运动员会给他们带来好运。如果高级别运动员抱起一个婴儿，那个孩子就可能长得高大、强壮。相扑运动员很受女士们的青睐，通常他们和模特、演员或电视明星结婚。

---

diabete *n.* 糖尿病   calorie *n.* 卡路里（热量单位）

Who Is Stephen King?

Stephen King is one of the world's most famous writers. He has sold more books than any other American writer. His most popular works are horror, or *scary*, stories. But it isn't only his books that are popular. People all over the world line up to see the movies made from his books, movies like *Carrie, The Shining,* and *The Dead Zone.*

史蒂芬·金是谁?

史蒂芬·金是世界上最著名的作家之一，他的作品比美国其他任何一位作家的都畅销。他最流行的作品是恐怖或惊悚故事。不只是他的书流行，全世界的人都争相观看根据他的书拍成的电影，例如《凯莉》，《闪灵》以及《死亡地带》。

scary *adj.* 吓人的；使人惊慌的

Stephen King was born in 1947 in Portland, Maine. When he was two, his father *abandoned* the family. His mother had to take care of Stephen and his older brother alone. They moved from place to place because it was hard for his mother to find work. It was a difficult time, and they had little money. In the evenings, Stephen's mother read to him. His favorite story was *The Strange Case of Dr. Jekyl and Mr. Hyde*. Later, Stephen read the book himself. He wanted to write a story like it, but he wanted his story to be scarier. Stephen started to write his own stories when he was about seven. His mother always *encouraged* him and sent his stories to publishers. By age eighteen, Stephen published his first story.

Stephen graduated from high school in 1966 and went straight to college. He studied very hard and always worked in his free time to make extra money. King graduated in 1970. He wanted to be a

金1947年出生于缅因州的波特兰。他两岁的时候，父亲就离家出走了，母亲只能一个人照顾金和他的哥哥。由于妈妈找工作很困难，他们只能不停地搬家。那是段很艰难的日子，他们的钱很少。傍晚的时候，妈妈给金讲故事，他最喜欢的故事是《杰凯尔博士和海德先生奇案》。后来，金开始自己读书了。他想写一个像妈妈讲给他的那样的故事，但是他想让自己的故事更加恐怖。金七岁开始自己写故事，妈妈经常鼓励他把写好的故事送到出版商那里。18岁的时候，金便出版了他的第一部故事书。

金1966年中学毕业后直接进入了大学，他学习非常努力，并且他经常在课余时间打工赚钱。1970年金毕业后，他想当一名教师，但他却没

abandon v. 抛弃

encourage v. 鼓励

teacher, but he couldn't find work right away. He had to work at a gas station, then at a laundry service. King finally got a job teaching English at a private high school in Maine. That year Stephen married Tabitha Spruce, his college girlfriend. Tabitha was also a writer. They were happy, but they didn't have much money. They didn't even have a telephone!

King wrote a novel titled *Carrie*, but he thought no one would like it. This made him sad and angry, so he threw the book away. Tabitha saw him throw away all the pages and was also angry. She took the pages from the *trash*. She liked the story very much and thought other people would like it, too. She *persuaded* him to send his book to a publisher. Later, King got a telegram from the publisher. He read it and was shocked. They wanted to publish *Carrie*!

At first, bookstores sold only 13,000 copies of the book. Stephen

---

能很快找到工作，所以他只好先去加油站工作，而后又在洗衣房工作，终于他最后在缅因州的一家私立高中找到了一份英语教师的工作。那一年金与大学时的女友塔碧莎结婚，塔碧莎也是位作家。他们虽然很幸福，但却没有钱，甚至连一部电话也没有。

金写了一部叫《凯莉》的小说，但他认为没人会喜欢看这部小说，这令他感到既愤怒又悲伤，于是他把书扔到了一边。塔碧莎看到他扔了所有的书稿也感到非常生气，她把那些稿子从废纸篓里捡了回来。她非常喜欢这个故事，并且她认为别人也会喜欢。她说服金把书稿送到出版商那里。后来，金从出版商那里收到电报，金读完后感到震惊，他们想出版这本书！

起初，书店只卖了13,000本。金和塔碧莎都很高兴，但其他人却有更

---

trash *n.* 垃圾；废物　　　　　　　persuade *v.* 说服；劝说

and Tabitha were happy with that, but other people had bigger ideas. A company wanted to make a movie from the book, and Stephen agreed. After the movie, the book sold 3.5 million copies. The publisher told King he would earn $400,000. King couldn't believe it.

King immediately wanted to buy his wife a *fancy* present. He went to many stores on the way home, but everything was closed except the *drugstore*. He went in and looked for something nice to give Tabitha, but the drugstore didn't have fancy gifts. He wanted to bring her something, so he bought her a hair dryer.

Now that they had money from the book, Stephen and Tabitha didn't have to keep their jobs. They were both going to be full-time writers. Stephen King soon published more books and became rich and famous. He bought a big house in Maine for his wife and three children. It was a house that his wife always liked, but they couldn't

---

大的策划。一家公司想根据这个故事拍一部电影，金同意了。电影上映之后，书卖出了350万份。出版商告诉金，他将要赚到40万美金，这让金感到难以置信。

金立刻想去给他的妻子买一件梦想中的礼物。回家的路上他找了很多家店，但除了药店外都关门了。他走进去想给塔碧莎买点不错的礼物，但药店根本没有什么好的礼品。他只是想为她买点什么东西，最终他只买了个吹风机。

现在他们写书赚了钱，金和塔碧莎都不用工作了，于是他们都想成为专职作家。金很快出版了更多的书，金钱和名誉随之而来，他为妻子和3个孩子在缅因州买了一套大房子。这是他们一直梦想的，但在这之前是不可能的。那是一套拥有23个卧室的大房子，至今他们仍住在那里。金仍然

---

fancy *adj.* 别致的   drugstore *n.* 药房

afford it before his books became popular. It's an old house with twenty-three bedrooms. Today they live in the same house, and Stephen still works extremely hard. He works every day of the year except three: Christmas, the Fourth of July, and his birthday. He always writes six pages a day, and he usually works on two different books at the same time.

In June of 1999, King was in a bad *accident*. As he was walking along the road near his house, a *van* hit him. King had to have three operations on his legs and hips. People thought he might have to stop writing. It took a long time, but King recovered and continued with his work as usual. Does he ever think he will stop writing? He says he will stop when he can't find more stories—but Stephen King always finds more stories.

很努力地工作，一年之中他只有3天不用工作：圣诞节，国庆节和他的生日。他一般每天写6页，并且他通常同时进行两本书的创作。

　　1999年的6月，金遭遇了一场严重的车祸。当他在家附近的公路上散步时，一辆卡车把他撞倒在地。金的腿部和臀部做了三次手术，人们以为他可能会停止写作。虽然耽搁了很长的一段时间，金最终还是康复并且像以往一样继续工作。他想过要停止写作吗？他说当自己找不到题材时就会停止——不过他总能找到更多的题材。

---

accident *n.* 事故；意外　　　　　　　　　　　van *n.* 厢式货车

07

What Is the Story Behind the Bed?

People spend about one-third of their lives asleep. We can survive longer without food than without sleep. Sleeping is very important, so the bed is important. *Scientists* say that the first bed was probably some leaves. Now, of course, beds are much better than that, and we have lots of *choices*. An average bed today lasts about fifteen years, and

什么是床背后的故事?

人的一生中有三分之一的时间是用来睡眠的,人在不吃饭的情况下生存的时间要比不睡觉时坚持的时间更长。因此睡眠很重要,床也就很重要。科学家说最早的床可能就是树叶。当然,现在床的条件比那时好很多,而且我们现在可以有很多的选择。现在一般的床能用

scientist *n.* 科学家   choice *n.* 选择

most people change beds about five times in their life. Even with all the beds in the world, people still invent new ones. And some people are still searching for the perfect bed.

For most of human history, people slept on layers of cloth, palm leaves, or furs. They laid these on the floor. In ancient Egypt, over three thousand years ago, the *pharaohs* were the first to raise their beds off the floor. They slept on light beds made of wood. You could fold the bed and carry it. *Archaeologists* found beds like this in Tutankhamen's tomb. People back then did not think soft pillows were necessary. The Egyptians put their heads on headrests made of wood and the Chinese had ceramic headrests.

After the year 100, only the rich had beds. Poor people still slept on the floor. The bed became a symbol of wealth. One emperor of Rome had a silver bed. Beds were also a person's most valuable possession. When Shakespeare died, he gave his second best bed

---

十五年左右，一般人一生中大概要换五次床。现在世界上已经有了这么多的床，人们还是在不断地发明新床。有的人一直在寻觅最完美的床。

在人类历史发展的大部分时间，人们是睡在铺在地面上的布，棕榈叶或者兽皮上。在3000年前的古埃及，法老们首先把自己的床抬离地面。他们睡在由木头制成的轻巧的床上，这种床可以折叠并易于携带。考古学家在图坦卡门王的坟墓里发现了类似的床。那时的人不认为柔软的枕头是必要的，埃及人的枕头是木制的，而中国人的枕头则是陶瓷制的。

在公元100年以后，只有富人才有床，穷人仍然睡在地上。床成了财富的象征。罗马的一个皇帝有一张银床。床也是一个人最有价值的财产。莎士比亚去世的时候，把他第二好的床送给了妻子。床是如此的特别，以

---

pharaoh *n.* 法老；暴君　　　　　　archaeologist *n.* 考古学家

to his wife. Beds were so special that in England, when a rich person traveled to another person's home, he took his bed with him. When a person stayed at a hotel for the night, he had to share a bed with strangers. If a rich person came to the hotel, the manager threw a poor traveler out of a bed to make room. All this sharing meant that beds were not very clean, and insects lived in them. Some people, *especially* rich women, slept on a chair when they traveled.

After 1750, beds became beautiful pieces of furniture. They were made of carved wood. A beautiful bed at that time could cost $1 million in today's money. The beds had four posts, one on each corner. People used these to hang curtains around the bed. The curtains helped to keep the bed warm. Also, because you passed through one room to get to another, the curtains were good for *privacy*.

至于在英国，当一个有钱人到别人家旅居的时候也要带上自己的床。当一个人夜晚在旅馆过夜时，他不得不和陌生人共睡一张床。而当有钱人来到旅馆时，旅馆老板就会把穷人赶走给有钱人腾出地方。共睡一张床的后果就是床很脏，并且有很多的虫子。有些人，特别是一些富有的女士在旅行时宁愿睡在椅子上。

1750年之后，床成了一件美丽的家具。它们通常由木头雕刻而成，那时一张床的价格在今天要值一百万美元左右。床有四根柱子，每个角落一根，人们用这些柱子挂幔帐，幔帐能起到保暖的作用。而且，由于人们要穿过一间屋子才能去到另一间，因此幔帐也起到保护隐私的作用。

---

especially *adv.* 特别；尤其　　　　　　　　　privacy *n.* 隐私；私人空间

Beds also became higher and higher. Queen Victoria slept on a bed with seven *mattresses* on top of each other. She had steps beside the bed to reach the top. Mattresses usually had straw on the inside (for poor people) or feathers (for the rich). After 1820, people slept on cotton mattresses with metal springs inside them. Beds made of metal became popular, too. The best beds were made of a yellow metal called *brass*. Metal beds were better for your health than beds made of wood, because they had fewer insects in them. That's why hospital beds are metal today.

In ancient Rome, people slept in their everyday clothes. In England, people did not wear clothes in bed. They wore a cap to keep their head and ears warm. Later, men wore nightshirts and women wore long nightdresses and hats. It was only after 1890 that men started to wear *pajamas*.

床变得越来越高。维多利亚女王睡在有7张垫子的床上，她的床边有供她上下的台阶。在穷人家里，床垫里放的是草，而富人家里放的则是羽毛。1820年以后，人们睡在内部有弹簧的棉垫上。铁床也慢慢开始流行，最好的床是用一种叫作黄铜的黄色金属制成的。金属床比起木床来对人的健康更有利一些，因为他们很少生虫子。这也是为什么今天医院的床都是铁床的原因。

在古罗马，人们穿着衣服睡觉。在英国，人们在床上是不穿衣服的，他们戴帽子以保持头部和耳朵暖和。后来，男人们穿起了衬衫式长睡衣，女士们穿起了女式睡衣并戴帽子。直至1890年之后男人们才开始穿睡衣裤。

---

mattress *n.* 床垫   brass *n.* 黄铜
pajamas *n.* 睡衣

People had interesting ways to keep warm in bed. Many families shared one big bed. Some people had a small dog in bed to keep their feet warm. Sometimes, people warmed the bed before they got into it. They warmed stones, *wrapped* them in cloth, and put them in the bed. Later, they used bottles with hot water inside. One English Prime Minister, William Gladstone, filled his bottle with tea in case he was thirsty at night.

Some people in Asian cultures prefer to sleep on the floor. They sleep on a thick mattress of cloth layers called a *futon*. They can roll up the futon and put it away during the day. Some people put their futon on a low frame rather than on the floor. Then it looks a lot like a Western-style bed.

Beds today come in every size and shape. We have round beds, king-size beds, bunk beds, *adjustable* beds, waterbeds, airbeds, and futons. Are you feeling sleepy yet? Sweet dreams!

　　人们有些很有趣的床上保暖的方式。很多家庭全家人挤在一张大床上，有的人在床上放只小狗来给脚取暖。有时，人们在上床之前要先给床加温。他们先加热石头，把他们用布包起来放到床上。后来，人们开始用暖水瓶。一位英国的首相，威廉·格雷斯通，他在暖水瓶里放了茶叶以便在晚上口渴的时候饮用。

　　亚洲有些地方的人更喜欢睡在地上。他们睡在一种由布制成的叫作蒲团的厚垫子上。白天他们把蒲团卷起放到别处。有些人把蒲团放在矮架而不是地面上，这样看起来更像是西方风格的床。

　　今天的床有各种型号和形状。我们有圆床、巨无霸床、卧铺床、可调节的床、水床、气床和蒲团。现在感到有困意了吗？做个好梦吧！

---

wrap *v.* 包；缠绕　　　　　　　　　　　futon *n.* 蒲团；日式床垫
adjustable *adj.* 可调整的

How Did the Spanish Conquer the Aztecs?

Hundreds of years ago, there was a beautiful city on an island *in the middle of* a lake. It had buildings, roads, and palaces. In many ways, it was like London, which was the biggest city in the world at the time. But this city was thousands of miles away from London. It was the *capital* of the Aztec empire, an empire that controlled about six million people. It was the seat of government, the religious center, and the cultural center of Aztec life.

阿兹特克是如何被西班牙人占领的？

数百年以前，在一个湖心岛上有一座美丽的城市。城中有建筑、街道和宫殿，它在许多方面很像当时世界上最大的城市伦敦。但是这座城市距离伦敦有数千英里之遥。它就是阿兹特克帝国的首都。阿兹特克帝国当时掌控着600万人口。这座城市是阿兹特克帝国的政府所在地，它同时也是宗教和文化中心。这座城市就是特诺奇提特兰城，也就是

---

in the middle of 在……中间

capital *n.* 首都；省会

This beautiful city was Tenochtitlán. Today we call it Mexico City.

Hernán Cortés was a Spanish *explorer*. He left Spain when he was only nineteen to explore and settle the island of Cuba. But Cortés didn't want to live in Cuba. He wanted to explore and to be rich and famous. The Spanish government told him to explore what is today Mexico. Cortés was excited. He knew stories about the Aztecs. He heard the Aztecs had gold. In 1519, he and about 400 men sailed from Cuba to the coast of what is today Mexico. They were afraid. They heard stories that the Aztecs *sacrificed* people to their gods. And the Aztecs had an army of more than one million men. Cortés thought they didn't have a chance, but they got lucky—very lucky.

The Aztecs believed in many gods. One of the most terrible gods was Tezcatlipoca, or the Smoking Mirror. This god watched

---

今天的墨西哥城。

考第斯是一个西班牙探险者。19岁时他离开西班牙去探险，并移居了古巴岛。但考第斯并不想住在古巴，他想继续探险以变得出名和富有。西班牙政府让他去今天的墨西哥一带探险，他非常兴奋。他知道阿兹特克的故事，并听说阿兹特克有金子。1519年，他带了400人从古巴航行到今天的墨西哥海岸一带。他们有些恐惧，因为听说过阿兹特克人用活人祭祀神灵的故事。并且阿兹特克人有一支超过百万人的军队，考第斯认为虽然他们没有机会，但他们很幸运——并且非常幸运。

阿兹特克人相信很多神灵。他们最敬畏的神灵之一就是特兹特利波卡

---

explorer *n.* 探险家   sacrifice *v.* 祭献；牺牲

over the land and made the Aztecs powerful. Another of their gods was Quetzalcoatl, or the Feathered Serpent. They believed he lived in a strange land in the east across the sea. This god once came to earth as a white man with a black beard. He brought *knowledge* to the people, and the Aztecs liked him. This made the Smoking Mirror angry, so he forced the Feathered Serpent to go away. The Feathered Serpent promised to come back one day and become the ruler of the Aztecs. The Aztec priests predicted that the Feathered Serpent would come back during a special year on their calendar. That year was 1519.

In 1519, many strange things happened, like earthquakes. There was also a *comet*, which is a bright object that moves around the sun. People were waiting to see what would happen next. The emperor of the Aztecs was worried. He thought the Feathered Serpent would come and he would not be emperor anymore. Then

---

神，或者叫作冒烟的镜子。这个神守望着海岛，能让阿兹特克人更强大。另外一个神叫羽蛇。他们相信他住在东方海面上一个奇特的小岛上。这个神曾经以一个留着黑胡子的白人的形象来过人间。他给人们带来知识，所以阿兹特克人很喜欢他。这使得冒烟的镜子很恼怒，于是他命令羽蛇走开。羽蛇许诺有一天他会回来并成为阿兹特克的统治者。阿兹特克的巫师预言羽蛇会在他们日历上的一个特别的年份回来，那一年是1519年。

1519年，许多奇怪的事情发生了，比如地震，还有围绕太阳旋转的明亮的彗星。人们猜测接下来还会发生什么。阿兹特克的国王很焦虑，他认为羽蛇会回来，而他将不再是国王。这时他的人见到了考第斯，他长着

---

knowledge *n.* 知识；学问

comet *n.* 彗星

his men saw Cortés. He had white skin and a black beard, just like the Feathered Serpent, and he came from the east in the Feathered Serpent's special year. The biggest *coincidence* was that Cortés came to the Aztec empire on April 21. This was the day dedicated to the Feathered Serpent. This persuaded the Aztec emperor that Cortés was the Feathered Serpent. He sent his men to greet him and welcomed him to the city. He gave Cortés gifts of gold and jewels and gave him and his men a palace for their home.

Cortés and his men could not believe their luck. They didn't know about the many coincidences working in their favor. They took everything the Aztecs gave them. Soon they became arrogant and decided to take the city and the empire for Spain. They made the emperor their prisoner. *Meanwhile*, one of Cortés's men killed a group of Aztecs at a religious ceremony. All of this made the Aztecs very angry. Cortés tried to calm them down. He showed them their

---

白皮肤和黑胡子，正和羽蛇一样，而且他在预言羽蛇回归的特殊的年份从东方而来。更巧的是考第斯在4月21日到达了阿兹特克帝国，而这一天正是为羽蛇准备回归的日子。这使得阿兹特克国王相信考第斯就是羽蛇，他派人去迎接考第斯到了城市中。他送给考第斯黄金和珠宝作为礼物，还让考第斯和他的随从把宫殿当成自己的家。

考第斯和他的手下不敢相信自己的好运气，他们不知道是如此多的巧合帮了他们的忙。他们拿走了阿兹特克人送给他们的每件礼物。很快他们便变得骄傲自大起来，于是他们决定把这座城市和整个帝国献给西班牙。他们把阿兹特克国王变成了囚犯，同时，考第斯的人在一次宗教仪式上杀死了一批阿兹特克的人。所有这一切令其他的阿兹特克人非常恼怒，考第斯决定去安抚他们。他让他们看到了国王，但这并没起到什么作用。国王

---

coincidence *n.* 巧合　　　　　　　　　　　　　meanwhile *adv.* 同时

emperor, but this didn't help. The emperor got hurt and later died. Nobody knows who killed him. Then the Aztecs threw Cortés and his men out of the capital.

Cortés still wanted to *conquer* the city, so he came back two years later with his men. It was his second trip there. They and many natives who didn't like the Aztec government destroyed the palace and other buildings and killed many people. They took over the city and settled there. Cortés made the Aztec empire a *colony* of Spain. In 1820, that same land, Mexico, became an independent country.

Today, Mexico City is one of the biggest cities in the world. Many Mexicans are descendants of the Aztecs. More than one million Mexicans speak the Aztec native language, Nahuatl, as their first language. The old buildings and statues of the Aztecs mix with the modern buildings of Mexico City so that everyone remembers the city's rich history.

受了伤，而后便死去了，没有人知道是谁杀死了他。后来阿兹特克人把考第斯和他的人赶出了这座城市。

考第斯仍然想征服这座城市，两年后他们又回来了。这是他在这儿的第二次旅行，他们和许多不喜欢阿兹特克政府的当地居民一起摧毁了宫殿和其他的一些建筑，杀死了许多人。后来他们占领了城市，并在那里安了家，考第斯把阿兹特克帝国变成了西班牙的一个殖民地。1820年，阿兹特克帝国成了一个独立的国家。

今天，墨西哥城是世界上最大的城市之一。许多墨西哥人是阿兹特克人的子孙。有超过一百万的墨西哥人讲阿兹特克本土的语言——纳瓦特尔语。古老的阿兹特克的建筑与雕塑和墨西哥现代的建筑交相辉映，令每个人都会记住这座城市悠久的历史。

---

conquer *v.* 征服   colony *n.* 殖民地

Why Are the Williams Sisters Good at Tennis?

Venus and Serena Williams are two of the best *female* tennis players in the world. One expert said, "They're faster, stronger, and more powerful than any other women who play the game." But without their father to *guide* them, they probably would not know how to play tennis.

When Richard and Oracene Williams got married, Richard told

为何威廉姆斯姐妹擅长网球?

维纳斯和赛莲娜是世界上最优秀的两个女网球选手。一位专家说，"她们比世界上其他任何从事这项运动的女人都要迅捷和强壮。"但如果没有父亲的引导，她们可能都不知道如何去打网球。

当理查德和奥瑞西恩结婚时，理查德告诉他的妻子他想要5个女儿。1978年的时候，理查德看到一个女运动员在一场网球比赛中赢得了22,000美

---

female *n.* 女性；女人   guide *v.* 引导

42

his wife that he wanted to have five daughters. In 1978, Richard saw a woman win $22,000 in a tennis match. He decided he wanted his daughters to be tennis players, too. The three daughters he already had weren't interested in tennis, but Venus was born in 1980, and then Serena in 1981. Now he had five daughters and two more chances to have tennis players.

Richard Williams was not a *wealthy* man. He dropped out of high school at age sixteen. Then he and his wife started their family in Compton, California. This was not a nice place to live with a young family. "It was a dangerous neighborhood," said Richard. The only tennis courts were in a very bad area. Richard first taught himself to play, then he taught his two youngest daughters when they were about four years old.

Both girls liked tennis and were good at it. By age ten, Venus *appeared* on the front page of the *New York Times*. She was number

---

元，于是决定让自己的女儿也成为网球运动员，但他的3个女儿对网球不感兴趣。1980年维纳斯出生了，接着1981年赛莲娜出生了，现在他有了5个女儿并且其中两个有成为网球选手的可能。

理查德不是个富人，他16岁时就从高中辍学了。然后他和妻子在加州的康浦顿建立了家庭。这里并不是一个年轻家庭的理想居所。"附近的居住环境很危险"，理查德说。唯一的网球场在一块很糟糕的地方。理查德自己先学会了打网球，然后开始教两个4岁的小女儿打网球。

两个女孩都很喜欢网球并且打得很好。10岁时维纳斯开始出现在纽约时报的封面上，她是加州南部12岁以下女子组的冠军，赛莲娜也是10岁以下女

---

wealthy *adj.* 富有的

appear *v.* 出现；呈现

one in Southern California for girls under twelve years old. Serena was number one for girls under ten. Richard decided it was time to find a real trainer for Venus and Serena. He moved the family to Florida and *enrolled* the girls in a tennis school. They played tennis six hours a day, six days a week, and also took regular classes.

At age fourteen, Venus started to play in professional *tournaments* and won her first professional match. Now Venus was playing tennis with world-famous players. She got a lot of attention. The media was interested in her for many reasons: her age, her sister, her father, and her personal style. She was easy to recognize because of her unique hairstyle. She wore beads in her hair—1,800 beads, which took ten hours to put in. The next year, 1994, the Reebok shoe company paid Venus $12 million for a five-year contract to represent their products. That same year, Serena started to play professionally, too. She also

---

子组的第一名，理查德决定为赛莲娜和维纳斯聘请一位专业教练。他把家搬到了佛罗里达，并把两个女儿送进了网球学校。她们每天进行6小时的网球训练，每周6天，另外还上普通课程。

14岁的时候，维纳斯开始参加职业巡回赛并且取得了第一场职业比赛的胜利。现在维纳斯和世界著名的选手比赛，受到了广泛关注。媒体对她的关注出于多方面的原因：她的年龄，她的妹妹，她的父亲，还有她的个人风格，她独树一帜的发型很容易就被人们认出来。她的头发上戴满了珠子——1800个，这要花10个小时才能戴好。第二年，1994年，锐步鞋业公司支付给维纳斯120万美元并和她签了一份产品代言的五年期合同。同一年，赛莲

---

enroll *v.* 登记；使加入   tournament *n.* 锦标赛

wore beads in her hair. Later, Venus lost points in a tennis match because the beads from her hair fell all over the tennis court. After that, both sisters took out their beads.

Venus and Serena Williams are on the list of the top female tennis players in the world. Because of this, they sometimes have to play against each other professionally. Sometimes Venus wins; sometimes Serena wins. Sometimes they play together in doubles matches. A doubles match has two players on each side of the court. Each set of players works as a team against the other. Venus and Serena became the first sisters team to win a professional doubles match. The sisters went on to *represent* the United States in Sydney, Australia, for the Summer Olympics of 2000. They won a gold medal for doubles, then Venus won another gold medal on her own.

娜也开始踏入职业网坛，她的头发上也戴着小珠。后来，维纳斯因为头上的小珠在比赛中脱落撒满了全场而失分。自那以后，两姐妹都不戴头珠了。

维纳斯和赛莲娜都名列世界顶级女子网球选手的名单。因此，她们有时不得不在职业赛场上一决胜负。有时是维纳斯赢，有时是赛莲娜赢，有时她们在双打比赛中配合。双打比赛每方都有两名选手，两名选手组成团队互相配合和对方对抗。维纳斯和赛莲娜成为第一对赢得职业双打比赛的姐妹组合。姐妹俩接下来代表美国参加了在澳大利亚悉尼举行的2000年夏季奥运会并赢得了双打比赛的金牌，之后维纳斯赢得了自己的另一块金牌。

represent *v.* 代表

The sisters are similar to each other in their personalities and their *athletic* ability. Both of them are intelligent and get good grades in school. Their parents always made them spend as much time on schoolwork as on tennis. Venus still studies French and German and wants to learn Italian. She also writes *poetry* and works in the fashion industry. Serena speaks Russian and French. She gave a speech in French when she was in Paris. Both girls like to show what they know. They publish a *newsletter* called the Tennis Monthly Recap. Now they are thinking about college.

Venus and Serena Williams are great athletes who win tournaments and gold medals. They have made a lot of money and are very famous—you can even buy Venus and Serena dolls. But which sister is the better tennis player? We will see.

姐妹俩在性格和运动天赋上都有共同点。她们都很聪明，在学校的成绩也都不错。她们的父母经常让她们在学业上和网球上花同样的时间。维纳斯还在学习法语、德语并且打算学习意大利语。她也在写诗并且投身于时尚界。赛莲娜能说俄语和法语，她在巴黎时曾用法语发表演讲。两个女孩都愿意展示自己的学问。她们组办了一个名为网球每月回顾的新闻组，现在她们正考虑到大学进修。

维纳斯和赛莲娜是赢得职业巡回赛和奥运金牌的伟大运动员。她们名声大振，变得非常富有——你甚至可以买到和她们相同的玩偶。但谁是最优秀的网球运动员呢？我们拭目以待。

---

athletic *adj.* 运动的   poetry *n.* 诗
newsletter *n.* 时事通讯

10

Where Is Timbuktu?

Many people believe Timbuktu is a place of *mystery*. It is a romantic land from *legends*. People often use Timbuktu as a symbol of a place that is far away, unknown, or difficult to reach. For example:

"I want to work in this office, but my company may send me to Timbuktu."

"Sorry I'm late. I had to park my car in Timbuktu!"

蒂姆布克图在哪里？

许多人认为蒂姆布克图是一个神秘的地方，是一个传奇故事中的浪漫国度。人们经常把蒂姆布克图作为遥远、未知或者难以到达的地域的象征，例如：

"我想在这间办公室里办公，但我的公司把我派到了蒂姆布克图。"

"对不起，我迟到了。我不得不把车子停在蒂姆布克图了。"

---

mystery *n.* 神秘

legend *n.* 传奇；传说

"I'm happy that you like your gift. I had to go to Timbuktu to find it."

Timbuktu is not only a symbol. It is also a real place. It is a city in the country of Mali in western Africa. Timbuktu is on the edge of the Sahara Desert, about eight miles from the Niger River. Even today it is not easy to travel there; the best way to get there is by river or camel. At one time, Timbuktu was a very important city, like Rome, Athens, or Jerusalem. It was the center of learning in Africa, and people called it the "City of Gold."

A group of *nomads* created Timbuktu in the twelfth century. By the fourteenth century, it was a center for the gold and salt trade. Everyone needed salt, so they charged a high price for it. Sometimes, salt was more expensive than gold! People outside the *region* started to hear and talk about Timbuktu when Mansa Moussa was Mali's king. His religion was Islam, and he built

---

"我很高兴你喜欢你的礼物，我跑到蒂姆布克图才找到它。"

蒂姆布克图不仅是个符号，它同时也是个真实的地方。它是西非马里的一个城市。蒂姆布克图在撒哈拉大沙漠的边缘，距离尼罗河8英里。即使今天想到那里旅行也很困难，到那去最好的办法就是通过河流或者是骑骆驼。蒂姆布克图是个和罗马、雅典或耶路撒冷同等重要的城市，它是非洲文化知识的中心，被称为"金城"。

12世纪时一群流浪汉创建了蒂姆布克图。到了14世纪，它变成了黄金和食盐交易的中心。每个人都需要吃盐，因此他们把盐的价格定得很高。有时，食盐甚至比黄金的价格还高！当曼萨·莫萨成为马里的国王时，本地区外的人们开始听说和谈论起蒂姆布克图。莫萨信仰伊斯兰教，

---

nomad *n.* 流浪者；游牧民   region *n.* 地区

beautiful *mosques* and huge libraries to spread the religion. Timbuktu was also famous for its universities. The University of Sankore had 25,000 students. People called it the Oxford University of the Sahara. Moussa made Timbuktu into a cultural center for Islam. It became an important city not just in Africa, but also in the world of Islam.

Stories about the wealth of Timbuktu spread far and wide, and other *kingdoms* wanted it for themselves. In 1591, Morocco conquered Timbuktu and controlled it until 1780. During this time, they killed many of the students and teachers, closed the universities, destroyed trade, and did not take care of the city. Timbuktu was no longer the City of Gold. After the Moroccans, other African groups controlled Timbuktu.

In the late eighteenth and early nineteenth centuries, European countries began to make colonies in some parts of Africa. Europeans believed Timbuktu was a city covered in gold. They thought gold

---

他修建了许多漂亮的清真寺和巨大的图书馆用于传播宗教。蒂姆布克图也因它的大学闻名。圣克莱大学有25,000名学生，人们把它称作是撒哈拉沙漠的牛津大学。莫萨使得蒂姆布克图变成了伊斯兰的文化中心。它不仅变成非洲重要的城市，同样也是伊斯兰世界的重要城市。

关于蒂姆布克图财富的故事到处流传，另外一些王国也想把它据为己有。1591年，摩洛哥征服了蒂姆布克图并且一直控制到1780年。在这段时间内，他们杀死了许多学生和教师，关闭了大学，毁坏了贸易，并且弃城市于不顾。蒂姆布克图不再是金城。摩洛哥人走后，其他非洲部落控制了蒂姆布克图。

在18世纪末和19世纪初，欧洲国家开始在非洲建立殖民地。欧洲人相信蒂姆布克图是一个遍地黄金的城市。他们认为在那里黄金和沙子一样

---

mosque *n.* 清真寺   kingdom *n.* 王国

in Timbuktu was as common as sand! Europeans tried to reach Timbuktu again and again, but they weren't successful. They didn't know how to cross the Sahara Desert and survive where it was hot and there was no water. The men died of *thirst* and disease, or thieves killed them.

In 1824, The Geographical Society of Paris offered a prize of 100,000 francs to the first person who could bring back information about Timbuktu. Many people tried, but René Caillié was the first to reach Timbuktu and come back alive. He started on the coast of western Africa and traveled for a year. On the way, he learned to speak Arabic and dressed as an Arab. He finally arrived in Timbuktu in April 1828, but he couldn't believe his eyes. He saw a city of small houses made of earth—no buildings covered with gold. The *economy* of Timbuktu was dead, but the intellectual and religious life of the city continued to live. When the French colonized the area in 1894, more

---

普通。欧洲人一次又一次尝试到达蒂姆布克图，但都失败了。他们不知道如何在酷热并且没有水的条件下穿越撒哈拉大沙漠还能生存，那些人都死于饥渴和疾病，或者被强盗杀死。

1824年，巴黎地理协会悬赏100,000法郎给第一个带回有关蒂姆布克图的消息的人。许多人尝试过，但瑞尼·凯历是第一个到达蒂姆布克图并活着回来的人。他从非洲的西海岸出发，整整旅行了一年。在路上，他学会了说阿拉伯语并且着装也像一个阿拉伯人。他最终在1828年4月到达了蒂姆布克图，但他不敢相信自己的眼睛，眼前只有一座由小土房构成的城市，并没有任何建筑覆盖着金子。蒂姆布克图的经济已经停滞了，但这座城市的文化和宗教生活依然延续。当1894年法国殖民者占领这片土地

---

thirst *n.* 渴；口渴

economy *n.* 经济

than twenty schools were still open and were doing very well.

Mali became an independent country in 1960. It is a poor country, and Timbuktu is a poor city. Some of the beautiful old buildings are still standing. Sankore University is still open, but today it has only about 15,000 students. In 1974, the government of Mali and UNESCO built a center to hold and preserve over 20,000 old *documents* from Timbuktu's libraries. These documents were copied by hand over many centuries and contain more than a thousand years of knowledge. It is extremely important to preserve these documents, because Timbuktu is in danger. The sand and winds from the Sahara are destroying the plants, the water, and the *historic* buildings. There is now a program to save the city and its history. People don't want Timbuktu to become only a legend again.

Although it is hot, poor, and far away from everything, thousands of visitors come to this city of mystery every year.

时，仍有二十多所学校正常工作并且运行良好。

马里于1960年成为了独立国家。它是一个穷国，蒂姆布克图也是一个贫穷的城市。一些漂亮的古建筑仍然屹立，圣克莱大学仍然在运行，但今天它只有15,000名学生。1974年，马里的政府和联合国教科文组织成立了一个中心，用以收藏和保存蒂姆布克图图书馆的20,000份古文件。这些文件许多世纪以来都是手写相传，其中囊括了千年的文化。保存这些文件极其重要，因为蒂姆布克图处于危险的边缘。撒哈拉沙漠的风沙正在摧毁着这里的植物、水和历史建筑。现在有一项拯救这座城市和他的历史的计划，人们不想让蒂姆布克图再变成一个传说。

虽然蒂姆布克图很热，很穷，而且远离尘嚣，但每年还是有数以千计的人光临这座神秘之城。

---

document *n.* 文件；文书　　　　　　　　historic *adj.* 有历史意义的

Where Do the Most Vegetarians Live?

Some people choose to be vegetarian, but others are *vegetarian* because of their religion, their culture, or the place they live. There are vegetarians all over the world, but the country with the most vegetarians is India.

About one billion people live in India, and most follow the Hindu religion. Hindus think it is wrong to kill or make animals *suffer*.

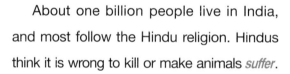

素食主义者通常住在哪里？

有些人自愿成为素食主义者，而有些人成为素食主义者则是由于他们的宗教、文化以及居住地。素食主义者遍及全世界，但人数最多的是在印度。

印度有十亿人，大多数信仰印度教。印度教认为杀死或虐待动物是错误的，他们认为如果这样做的话，将来有一天他们就会承受同样的痛苦。

vegetarian *n.* 素食者　　　　　　　　　　suffer *v.* 遭受；经受；忍受

They think if they do, they will suffer the same way one day. Hindus believe the cow is sacred; therefore, most Hindus do not eat beef. In fact, the Hindu word for cow, aghnaya, means "not to be killed."

There are different kinds of vegetarians in the world. Some vegetarians do not eat beef or red meat, but they eat chicken and fish. Some do not eat red meat, chicken, or fish but they eat *cheese*, butter, eggs, milk, and other animal products. Other vegetarians do not use anything that comes from an animal. Some don't wear wool because it harms the sheep, don't use silk because it hurts *silkworms*, and don't eat honey because they do not want to hurt bees. Other vegetarians only eat vegetables; however they do not kill plants. For example, they will not eat carrots or potatoes because when you pick them, the plant dies. They will eat apples or pears because picking them does not harm the plant. Some vegetarians do not kill

印度教人认为母牛是神圣的，因此，大多数印度教人不吃牛肉。实际上，印度教中牛这个词，aghnaya，意思是"不能被杀的"。

世界上有各种各样的素食者。有些人不吃牛肉或红肉，但他们吃鸡和鱼。有些人不吃红肉、鸡或鱼，但他们吃奶酪、黄油、蛋、牛奶和其他动物制品。另外一些素食者不用任何来自于动物身上的东西。有些人怕伤害绵羊不穿羊毛制品，怕伤害蚕不穿丝制品，怕伤害蜜蜂不吃蜂蜜。其他素食者只吃蔬菜，然而他们不伤害植物。比如，他们不吃萝卜和土豆，因为当你采摘它们的时候，它们的植株就会死。他们会吃苹果和梨，因为采摘

cheese　n.　奶酪　　　　　silkworm　n.　蚕；桑蚕

or hurt any animal—not even a fly or a mosquito!

In India, too, there are different kinds of vegetarians. Some Hindus are *strict* vegetarians. Other Hindus eat all meat except for beef, but they only eat it about once a week. Many families eat chicken or lamb a few times a year at special occasions, like weddings. The Hindus of the upper classes do not eat meat or drink *alcohol*. However, the lower classes eat all meats except for beef. The upper classes, or Brahmans, cannot kill anything that is moving. If they do, they believe they will become that animal in their next lives and will be killed, too.

Hindus follow other rules when they eat. They rinse their mouths, arms, and legs before and after eating to clean themselves. It is a custom for the man of the house to eat thirty-two mouthfuls at each

---

它们不会伤害到植株。一些素食者不杀死或伤害任何一种动物——甚至是苍蝇和蚊子。

　　印度的素食者的习俗也各不相同。有些印度教徒是严格的素食者，其他印度教徒除了不吃牛肉之外其他任何肉都吃，但是他们每周只吃一次。许多家庭每年在特殊的场合，比如婚礼上才吃鸡肉或者羊肉。上层社会的印度教人不吃肉，不喝酒。然而，下层社会的人吃除了牛肉外的所有肉类。上层阶级，或者叫Brahmans，不能杀死任何能移动的东西。如果他们这样做了，他们相信自己来生会变成动物并且同样被杀掉。

　　印度教人吃饭的时候还要遵从一些规则，在饭前和饭后冲洗自己的嘴，胳膊和腿来清洁自己。房主人每餐要吃三十二口，一边咀嚼一边思考

---

strict *adj.* 严格的　　　　　　　　　　　　　　alcohol *n.* 酒；酒精

meal, chewing carefully and thinking about pleasant things. Strict Hindus do not eat garlic or onions. They believe that foods have characteristics. Some foods are "hot," others are"cold." They think the strong smells of these foods are too powerful for the *mild* tastes and smells of other vegetables. Also, in middle-class families, many women do not eat meat, but men do. Women think eating meat is something *masculine*. They also connect meat with violence.

Hindus also think it is lucky to eat with a person who is one hundred years old or a student, but should avoid eating with a bald person, an actor, an athlete, a musician, or a woman with a second husband. Strict Hindus also believe it is not correct for a wife to eat with her husband, but it is good if she eats the rest of his food after he finishes his meal. It is wrong for a Hindu to eat food that has stood overnight, has been cooked twice, or is left over from an

---

愉快的事情是一种传统。严格的印度教徒是不吃蒜或洋葱的。他们相信食物也有特性，有些食物是"热"的，有些则是"凉"的。他们认为这些食物强烈的味道对于其他味道温和的植物来说太霸道了。同样，在中产阶级的家庭中许多妇女是不吃肉的，但是男人吃。妇女认为吃肉是很男性化的举动，她们还把吃肉和暴力联系在一起。

印度教也认为和一位百岁老人或者和学生共同进餐是幸运的，但他们会避免和光头的人、演员、运动员、音乐家或者二婚的女人共同进餐。严格的印度教徒也认为妻子和丈夫共同进餐是不对的，但他们觉得丈夫用餐完毕后妻子去吃剩下的食物是良好的行为。印度教人认为吃隔夜的食物，两次烹饪的食物或者前次剩下的食物是不好的。任何被人的脚、衣服或者

---

mild *adj.* 温和的；温柔的　　　　　　masculine *adj.* 男性的；男子气概的

earlier meal. Any food that has been touched by a foot, a person's clothing, or a dog cannot be eaten.

Vegetarians are everywhere in both rich and poor countries. In parts of the world such as Africa, the Middle East, and Southeast Asia, meat is uncommon, and therefore it is an easy choice to be vegetarian. Surveys show that in both the United States and Britain about 4 percent of the *population* is vegetarian. And more and more people are choosing *vegetarianism* every day. Many people become vegetarian for health reasons. They look and feel better when they stop eating meat. Some famous vegetarians include Leonardo da Vinci, Albert Einstein, Thomas Edison, Leo Tolstoy, Brad Pitt, Sylvester Stallone, Paul McCartney, Penelope Cruz, and Madonna.

狗碰过的食物都是不能吃的。

素食者到处可见，无论在穷国还是富国。在世界的某些地方，比如非洲、中东和东南亚，肉类是不常见的，因此很容易成为素食者。调查显示在美国和英国大约有4%的人口是素食者，并且每天都有更多的人选择成为素食者。许多人选择素食是出于健康的原因。当他们不吃肉以后看起来感觉好多了，一些素食的名人包括达·芬奇、爱因斯坦、爱迪生、托尔斯泰、布拉德·皮特、史泰龙、保罗·迈卡蒂、潘尼洛甫·克鲁兹和麦当娜。

---

population *n.* 人口　　　　　　　　vegetarianism *n.* 素食主义

What Is the Legend **o**f King Arthur?

The legend of King Arthur and the Knights of the Round Table makes us think of an age of heroism and romance. For a thousand years, stories about them have been passed down from *generation* to generation, across Europe and the rest of the world. We even *encounter* them today in books, on television, and in the movies. In all these stories, King Arthur and his knights fight bravely for justice

---

亚瑟王的传奇

亚瑟王的传奇和圆形竞技场的骑士令我们想起那个充满英雄气息和浪漫的时代。几千年来，他们的故事在欧洲和世界的其他地方广为流传。即使在今天的书本、电视和电影中我们也能找到他们的身影。在这些故事中，亚瑟王和他的骑士们为了正义和真理而英勇奋战，当然几乎每次他们都是胜利而归。

---

generation *n.* 一代人　　　　　　　　encounter *v.* 意外遇到；邂逅

and truth. Of course, they always win.

The legendary King Arthur was known as the greatest king that ever lived. His magnificent castle was called Camelot, and his wife, Guinevere, was the most beautiful woman in history. Arthur had the greatest *knights* at his court. They were all equal and sat at a round table to show that no one had a higher rank than the other. The most famous knights were Sir Gawain and Sir Lancelot. The knights did many good deeds and went on adventures. They saved young women in trouble and searched for a precious cup called the Holy Grail. They were all heroes, although they had faults like all people do.

In the legend, Arthur is the perfect king. He has a *wizard* by the name of Merlin who helps him *defeat* his enemies. He also has flashing swords and wears a fine suit of shining *armor*. Arthur has two magic swords. At the beginning of his reign, he pulls one from a block of stone, proving that he is the true king. The other sword

---

具有传奇色彩的亚瑟王被认为是迄今为止最伟大的国王，他宏伟的城堡被称作卡米洛城，他的妻子基尼维尔皇后是有史以来最漂亮的女人。他的手下有最英勇的骑士，他们都是平等的。他们围坐一张圆桌以示地位平等。最有名的武士是高文和莱斯罗。这些武士平日总做好事，还善于冒险，经常救妇女于危难中。他们还寻找一只被称为圣杯的珍贵杯子。尽管他们像其他人一样有缺点，但他们都是英雄。

在传说中，亚瑟王是个十全十美的国王。他有个叫莫林的巫师帮助他战胜敌人。他佩两把闪光的魔剑和一身闪亮的盔甲。那两把魔剑中的一把

---

knight *n.* 骑士；武士
defeat *v.* 击败；战胜

wizard *n.* 男巫
armor *n.* 盔甲

appears in the middle of a lake and has powers that make Arthur immortal. At the end of his reign, Arthur returns to the lake and disappears into the mist.

Are these stories true? Did King Arthur really exist? Was his wife, Guinevere, real? Did Camelot exist? How true to fact are some of these stories? Historians don't know. For the last few hundred years, people thought that the legend about Arthur had been *invented*. However, historians have realized recently that Arthur really may have existed. Most historians believe that he probably did. They think that he was a king or a great leader somewhere in Great Britain. Most believe that Arthur lived around the end of the fifth and beginning of the sixth *century*. They also believe that he led an army against the Saxons who invaded Britain a very long time ago, that he won this great battle, and that he was the character who inspired hundreds of stories.

是在他统治初期，从一堆石头中拔出来的，以证明他是真命天子。另一把是在湖中间，它的力量能使国王不朽。统治结束时，他就回到了这个湖，消失在迷雾中。

这些故事是真的吗？亚瑟王真的存在吗？他的妻子基尼维尔皇后真的存在吗？这些故事的可信度有多少？历史学家也搞不清。在过去的几百年中，人们认为亚瑟王的传说是编造出来的。但最近历史学家认为亚瑟王确实存在过。他们认为他曾经是英国某地的国王或领导人。许多人都说他生活在大约五世纪末六世纪初，领导士兵与早期侵略英国的撒克逊人抗衡，最后取得了战争的胜利。人们根据他创编了几百个传奇故事。

---

invent *v.* 虚构；创作   century *n.* 世纪；百年

The stories about Arthur may have some truths in them, but they also have a lot of *exaggerations*. It seems difficult to separate fact from *fiction*. Some people question how a man could win so many battles and sword fights without getting wounded or killed. And some of the things that Arthur's adviser Merlin says and does are too fantastic to be real. For example, he made predictions of strange and amazing things that would happen in the future, and many stories claim that he could change himself into different objects and animals. He could change into a boy or a deer, for example, and he could change the appearance of others and even make them invisible. However, there are other parts of the stories we accept more easily, such as the magnificent castle of Camelot with its many towers.

There have been various theories about where Camelot was located and whether it even existed. In the late 1960s, historians dug

---

亚瑟王的故事具有一定的真实性，但也有一些夸张，真假似乎很难分辨。有些人质疑他如何能成功地赢得这么多场战争。他的顾问莫林所说的或所做的事让人觉得太不可思议，无法相信。比如，他对将来发生的许多奇怪的事做了预测，在许多故事中，他声称能把自己变成不同的事物或动物。他能变成一个小男孩或一头鹿，还能改变别人的相貌或使他们隐身。但有关他的其他故事我们还是能够接受的，比如有许多宝塔的宏伟的卡米洛城等。

关于卡米洛城是否存在以及它的位置究竟在哪儿有多种说法。六十年代末期，历史学家在英国东北部那个被认为是卡米洛城的所在地向下挖，

---

exaggeration *n.* 夸张；夸大　　　　　　　fiction *n.* 虚构；杜撰

at a site in southeastern England(Cadbury Castle) where *Camelot* could have been located, but they found nothing. Some historians say that big stone castles didn't exist in the time of Arthur. Castles during his time were made of dirt and stone, and they were nothing like the castle described in the stories.

Still, the idea of Camelot as a wonderful, perfect place continues. In the 1960s, there was a popular musical show called Camelot that said that life was perfect in Arthur's castle. Today in the English language, the word Camelot has come to mean an ideal place. It is often *associated* with President John F. Kennedy's White House years, because his presidency started a new "golden age" of *prosperity* in the United States.

Most of the stories about King Arthur were written in the ninth century and later. The stories tell us about the people and values of

---

结果什么也没有发现。有的历史学家认为那个巨大的石头城堡在亚瑟王时期根本就不存在。那个时期的城堡是用泥土和石头建的，根本就不像故事里所描述的那样。

但卡米洛城是个胜地这种说法一直延续着，六十年代流行的歌谣"卡米洛城"就认为城堡的生活非常完美。今天，英语单词Camelot就是仙境的意思。这个单词还经常和开创了美国黄金时代的约翰·肯尼迪联系在一起。因此他的统治是美国繁荣时期一个新的"黄金时代"。

很多关于亚瑟王的故事都是从公元9世纪以来写成的，向人们讲述了那段时期的人们及其价值观。许多都是关于荣誉和骑士精神的，亚瑟王和

---

associate *v.* 联系   prosperity *n.* 繁荣；昌盛

these times. Most of them talk about a code of honor, or chivalry. King Arthur and his knights were all chivalrous. They respected others. A chivalrous person did not kill his enemy after the enemy surrendered. Arthur and his knights were expected to show respect for the church and pity for the poor, as well as bravery and courtesy.

The most famous *version* of King Arthur's legend, a book called *Morte d'Arthu (Death of Arthur)*, was written by Sir Thomas Malory in the fifteenth century. In his work, Malory creates a story of *extraordinary* bravery and emphasizes the *triumph* of good over evil. This work inspired kings all over Europe. King Henry VIII of England saw himself as the new Arthur reuniting the country after civil war, and even naming his eldest son Arthur.

King Arthur's popularity is ongoing. In 1986, it was estimated that 13,500 books, articles, and reviews had been written about him. The success of recent movies and books shows that the popularity of

---

他的骑士都很勇敢正直，尊敬他人。一个有骑士精神的人在敌人投降后是不会杀他的。人们希望亚瑟王和他的骑士不仅尊重教堂，同情贫苦人民，还希望看到他们勇敢，有礼貌。

关于亚瑟王的传说最有名的是《亚瑟王之死》，是托玛斯·马洛里爵士在15世纪时写成的。在这部作品中，他讴歌了亚瑟王非凡的勇敢并强调正义必将战胜邪恶。这部作品使所有欧洲的国王受到了极大的鼓舞，英国的亨利八世把自己看成是内战后归来的新亚瑟王，他甚至给自己的大儿子起名叫亚瑟。

亚瑟王的故事一直深受大家的喜爱。截止到1986年，据估计，关于他的书籍和文论已达13,500部之多。最近一些电影和书籍的广泛流行也证明他的影响力在当今仍然是相当大的。为什么呢？亚瑟王的故事是一个冒

---

version *n.* 版本
triumph *n.* 胜利

extraordinary *adj.* 非凡的

the legend of King Arthur is still strong today. Why is this? The story of Arthur is an adventure story. There are sword fights and wars that make the story exciting. There is also romance, and the setting is far away and *exotic*. The themes in the stories are universal: the fight between good and evil, the conflict between love and duty. Another theme in the stories shows that although Arthur is a king, he makes mistakes and, like all people, he is not perfect. He is, in fact, like us in many ways. Maybe it is this *combination* of greatness and humanness that has made King Arthur a popular figure around the world and throughout history.

险故事，里面的很多剑战场面非常精彩。还有很多浪漫的故事，其背景也颇具异国风情。这些故事的主题都是一致的：正义与邪恶的斗争，爱与责任的冲突。故事的另一个主题是尽管亚瑟是个国王，但他像其他人一样，也不是完人，也会犯错误。事实上，在很多方面他都跟我们很相似。也许正是这种伟大与平常的结合使他成为历史上广受欢迎的人物。

---

exotic *adj.* 异国情调的   combination *n.* 联合；结合

13

Why Did the Inca Empire Disappear?

The land of the Incas included what is now Bolivia, Peru, Ecuador, and part of Argentina and Chile. In the center of the Inca *Empire* was its capital, Cuzco, the "Sacred City of the Sun". From every part of the empire, grain, gold and silver, cloth, and food *poured* into the capital.

The Incas began as a small tribe

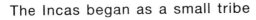

印加帝国的消亡

印加帝国包括今天的玻利瓦尔，秘鲁，厄瓜多尔和阿根廷的一部分以及智利。在印加帝国的中部是它的首都库斯科——太阳下的圣城。帝国各地的谷物，黄金，白银，布料和食物都涌进首都。

大约在1100年左右，印加人在安第斯山脉的小部落起家。到了1300

empire *n.* 帝国   pour *v.* 涌流

living in the Peruvian Andes in the 1100s. In the 1300s, their strong leader, Mayta Qapaq, began to *conquer* neighboring lands. By the 1400s, the Incas' huge empire became the largest empire known in the Americas. Although there were only 40,000 Incas, they ruled a population of about 12 million, which included 100 different peoples. The Incas were clever *governors* and did not always force their own ideas on other groups. The people they conquered had to accept the Inca gods, but they were allowed to *worship* in their own way and keep their own customs.

Each new ruler of the empire was called the Sapa Inca, and each Sapa Inca claimed to be the child of the sun and was treated as a god. When a Sapa Inca died, his body was kept and taken care of by the people, and he continued to "live" in his palace. The dead Inca sat on a golden stool, and a woman watched him day and night, whisking the flies away from his face. The dead rulers were

---

年左右，他们英勇的领导人梅塔·夸帕克开始侵略周边的国家。到1400年，印加帝国已经成为美洲最大的帝国。尽管他们只有4万人口，但他们却统治着120万人，包括100个不同的种族。印加人是非常精明的统治者，他们很少把自己的想法强加于别人。被征服者必须接受印加人所信仰的神，但允许他们以自己的方式进行崇拜，也允许他们保持自己的传统。

　　每一个新的统治者都被称作国王，每个国王都被认为是太阳之子，人们像对待上帝一样对待他们。当国王死后，人们会保存好他们的尸体，就好像他仍然生活在宫殿一样。死去的印加国王坐在黄金塑的凳子上，有个女人日夜看守着他，驱赶飞到他脸上的苍蝇。死去的统治者每天仍有食物供应，在

---

conquer *v.* 战胜；征服　　　　　　　　　　　governor *n.* 统治者
worship *v.* 崇拜

served food each day, and on special occasions they were carried out of their palaces to feast together. Each new ruler had to build a new palace. By 1500, Cuzco was full of palaces of dead Incas.

Each Sapa Inca had a queen, or Coya. She was almost always the ruler's own sister. Like him, she was thought to be a child of the sun. The Sapa Inca married his sister to make sure their children only had the pure blood of the sun. One of their sons would be the next Sapa Inca. However, each Sapa Inca had many *unofficial* wives and dozens of children who would become the Inca *nobility*.

The Incas ruled over one of the best organized empires in history. They controlled the lives of everyone through a system of officials. This system was like a triangle or pyramid. At the bottom were millions of ordinary farmers. Above the farmers were officials and higher officials, and above these officials were the four governors of the quarters of the empire. At the very top of the pyramid was the Sapa Inca.

特殊的日子里，他们还会被抬出宫殿参加宴会。每个继承王位的国王都会修座新宫殿。到1500年，库斯科已经到处是死去的印加国王的宫殿。

　　每个国王都会有个王后或叫克亚，通常都是统治者自己的姐妹。就像国王一样，她也被认为是太阳的孩子。国王娶他的姐妹是为了确保他们的孩子是纯太阳血统。新的国王一般在这些孩子中产生。但每个印加国王都有许多非正式的妻子和几十个孩子，这些孩子都成为印加的贵族。

　　印加人统治的这个帝国是历史上最有组织性的帝国之一。他们通过一套官僚系统控制着每个人的生活，这套系统像个三角形或金字塔。在最底层的是普通农民。农民之上是官员或高级官员。在这些官员之上是帝国四个辖区的领导人，金字塔最顶端的是印加国王。

---

unofficial *adj.* 非正式的　　　　　　　　　　　　nobility *n.* 贵族

Ordinary people had to spend part of each year working for the state—mining, buildings roads, or serving in the army. They could not leave their villages without official *permission*. They had no choice but to work on the land and send one-third of their produce to the government stores. The empire had huge storehouses where food was kept. The Incas made sure no one starved. In return, everyone was expected to work.

Even marriage of the ordinary people was controlled. Although nobles often had several wives, an ordinary man could only have one. The state controlled whom and when each ordinary person could marry. Each year the local chiefs assembled all the *eligible* young men over twenty-four and women over eighteen. They were grouped into two lines and then paired together. For the first year of marriage, the couple did not have to pay taxes on either goods or labor. However, they would have to work hard for the rest of their

---

普通人需要在一年中抽出点时间来为国家工作，比如采矿、修路或从军。没有官方的许可，他们不许离开村庄。所以他们别无选择只能耕地，然后把三分之一的收获上交国库。帝国修有巨大的仓库来保存粮食。印加帝国确保没人饿死，反过来，他们也要求每个人都得工作。

就连平民的婚姻也是有限制的。尽管贵族都有好几个妻子，但平民只能有一个。国家掌控着平民跟谁结婚以及什么时候结婚。每年，地方官把满24岁的小伙和满18岁的姑娘集合在一起，他们分别站成两排然后进行配对。结婚的第一年，新婚夫妇不用交纳物品税和劳力税。但他们必须努

---

permission *n.* 允许；许可 　　　　　eligible *adj.* 合格的；符合条件的

lives. When they were elderly and became too frail or sick to take care of themselves, they received free food and clothes from the state storehouse, and their family group would care for them.

The Incas had no horses or wheels to help them with transportation, but they had a *sophisticated* road system. Their network of roads ran the length of the empire, from today's Peru to Chile. One road, called the Royal Road, was 3,250 miles (5,200 km) long. It was built through the Andes Mountains. Even today, with modern tools, it would be difficult to build that road. The Incas also made *extraordinary* suspension bridges of ropes; these hung 300 feet (91 meters) above deep rivers. Since most people were not allowed to travel, the roads were used by soldiers and chasquis, who were government messengers. They were highly trained runners who were stationed at intervals of about two mile (3.2 km) along the roads and carried messages to and from Cuzco, the capital. Relay teams could

力工作，等到老了或生病不能自理时，他们就会得到国库免费提供的食物和衣服，家族的成员也可以照顾他们。

印加国没有马或车帮助他们运输，但他们有一套精密的道路系统，覆盖全国，从今天的秘鲁到智利，其中有一条被称作皇家大道的路，全长5200千米。这条路横跨安第斯山脉。即使在今天，运用现代化工具修建这条路也很费劲。印加人还修建了壮观的绳索吊桥。桥到深水的距离有91米。由于国家不允许人们到处旅游，所以这些路是只为士兵和政府信差修建的。这些人都经过集中训练，每隔3.2千米就有人驻守，他们负责把信

sophisticated *adj.* 复杂的；高级的   extraordinary *adj.* 非凡的

run up to 200 miles(322 km) a day and bring fish from the sea to the capital in two days. But the main reason for the roads was for the soldiers who kept the empire under control.

Although they had no system of writing, the Incas sent messages in quipus, which were colored strings with *knots* in them. The color of the string represented what was being counted. For example, a yellow string *stood for* gold and a red string for soldiers. The knots stood for numbers.

The Incas were expert builders, although they only had basic tools. Instead of building walls with cement, they used stones that fit together perfectly. Many of the Inca walls remain in place to this day. In 1950, two-thirds of Cuzco was destroyed in an earthquake, but none of the old walls collapsed. Today the well-preserved town of Machu Picchu shows the remarkable skills of the Inca builders. This town, which was *abandoned* by the Incas for unknown reasons, was

---

息传出或传入首都。邮递组合一天能跑322千米，能在两天内把鱼从海边送到首都。但修路的主要目的是要掌控整个帝国。

尽管没有书写系统，但他们用"奎普斯"即有颜色的绳打成绳结来传递信息。绳的颜色代表着某种特定事物。比如，黄色的绳代表黄金，红色的绳代表士兵，绳结代表数字。

印加人尽管只有最基本的工具，但他们是建筑的能手。他们把石头完美地拼合在一起，而不是用水泥砌墙。许多印加时期的墙还完整地保存到今天。1950年，一场地震摧毁了库斯科三分之二的建筑，但没有一面墙倒塌。至今仍保存完整的马丘·比丘镇就展示了印加人精湛的技术。这个

---

knot *n.* （绳索等的）结

abandon *v.* 放弃

stand for 代表；象征

only discovered in 1911.

The Inca Empire fell very quickly after the death of their great ruler Huayna Capac in 1525. Two of his sons, Atahualpa and Huascar, quarreled over who should be the next Sapa Inca. They fought against each other in a war and finally, in 1532, Atahualpa won. During the war, news came that strange people had arrived on the *coast*. These visitors, the Spaniards, were dressed in metal suits, rode unknown animals(horses), and had hair growing down their chins. After his victory, Atahualpa wanted to see these strange people and invited them to visit him. There were only 180 Spaniards, so Atahualpa was not afraid. However, the Spaniards attacked the Inca army with guns and fired their cannons. They took Atahualpa prisoner and promised to give him his freedom *in exchange for* a room full of gold and two rooms full of silver. The Incas gave the Spaniards the gold and silver. However, the Spaniards didn't free Atahualpa;

当时不知为何被人遗弃的小镇到1911年才被发现。

1525年印加国王加巴克逝世后，印加帝国很快瓦解。他的两个儿子阿塔胡亚尔帕和华思卡为继承王位争执不已，最后发展到了血腥的战争。1532年阿塔胡亚尔帕赢得了战争的胜利。在这期间，有消息说有异族人登陆，这些西班牙人穿铁盔，骑着他们不认识的动物（马），脸颊上还长着头发。阿塔胡亚尔帕取胜后，想会见这些人，就发出了邀请。那时只有180个西班牙人，阿塔胡亚尔帕并不担心，但是这些西班牙人却用枪攻打军队，并且开炮。他们把阿塔胡亚尔帕关进监狱并提出换取自由的条件：一屋黄金，两屋白银。印加人满足了他们的条件。但是，他们却没有释放

---

coast n. 海岸　　　　　　　　in exchange for 以……来交换

they killed him instead. With no leader, the Inca soldiers were weak, and the Spaniards soon defeated them. The Spaniards gave the Incas orders, and the Incas obeyed them because they were used to obeying all their lives. The Spaniards were only interested in the Inca gold and silver, so they made the people work in the mines and *neglect* the farming. Many Incas died from overwork and hunger. The great Inca Empire was soon destroyed.

Though the Inca civilization disappeared, traces of its culture and people survive. As a matter of fact, today the Incas' *descendants* form the majority of the population in the Andes of Ecuador, Peru, and Bolivia.

阿塔胡亚尔帕,反而把他杀了。群龙无首,印加士兵如一盘散沙,迅速被西班牙人击败。西班牙人对他们发号施令,他们已习惯听别人的差遣,所以就遵从这些命令。西班牙人只对他们的金银感兴趣,于是又把他们赶去开矿而忽视了农业生产。许多印加人由于过度疲劳和饥饿而死亡,印加帝国迅速瓦解。

尽管印加文明消失了,但文化的痕迹却保留下来了,人们也生存下来了。事实上,今天安第斯山脉的厄瓜多尔、秘鲁和玻利维亚的大多数人口都是印加帝国的后裔。

---

neglect *v.* 忽视;疏忽   descendant *n.* 后裔;子孙

14

How Do Hindus Celebrate the Diwali Festival?

Diwali is the Hindu festival of light. The Hindus in India celebrate their favorite *festival* on the dark and cold nights of late October or early November. Diwali, which is short for dipawali, means "row of lights". There are lights everywhere during this festival, which is as important to Hindus as Christmas is to *Christians*. Houses have

印度人是如何庆祝排灯节的?

排灯节是印度的灯节。印度人在十月底或十一月初漆黑又寒冷的夜晚庆祝他们喜欢的节日。排灯是dipawali的简称,是"光线"的意思。节日期间到处都是灯,它对印度人而言,就好像是圣诞节对基督教徒那么重要。门前窗上到处都是灯,大街也被灯点缀得很美丽,

---

festival *n.* 节日   Christian *n.* 基督徒

lights in front of their doors and windows, the streets are *decorated* with lights, and the temples have tiny rows of lights all over. Diwali, which lasts for five days, is one of the longest festivals for Hindus. In India, it's a time when everything stops. Families get together, eat together, and exchange gifts, usually of candies. They go shopping and buy things, from new clothes to new homes.

As with other Indian festivals, Diwali has different *significance* for people in various parts of India, depending upon which gods the people worship at this time. However, the basic reason for this festival is the same all over India: Diwali is a time for new beginnings. It is a time when light triumphs over darkness and good triumphs over evil.

Before celebrating Diwali, Hindus prepare and decorate their homes. People make sure that their houses are spotless. Every

---

寺庙里也一直有微弱的灯光。排灯节一共持续5天，是印度最长的节日之一。这几天整个国家的各行各业都停止工作，家庭进行聚餐，并交换礼物，通常是蜡烛。他们还去购物，包括购买新衣服、新房等。

相对其他节日，排灯节对印度各地的人们来说有着不同的意义，这取决于当时人们所信仰的神。但目的都是一样的：排灯节是新生活的开始，这一时刻意味着人们用光明战胜黑暗，正义战胜邪恶的信念。

在庆祝活动开始前，印度人便着手装饰自己的家。他们要确保房屋一尘不染。每家每户都重新粉刷，彻底打扫。他们在房屋的地板和侧廊里喷

---

decorate *v.* 装饰；修饰   significance *n* 意义；重要性

house is repainted and thoroughly cleaned. They decorate the floors and sidewalks outside their homes with special rangoli patterns to welcome guests. Rangoli means "a mixture of colors". The patterns are created from a paste made from rice flour. The paste is usually colored red or yellow. The Hindus believe red and yellow make the evil spirits go away. One traditional Hindu pattern is the *lotus* flower, which is the symbol of one of their gods, Lakshmi.

Lights play an important part in the Diwali festival. Weeks before the festival, potters make clay lamps called diwas. On the first day of Diwali, every family buys a new lamp, which *symbolizes* new beginnings. There are lights everywhere in the streets. Even in parts of India where there is no electricity, thousands of these clay lamps can be seen. The lamps welcome travelers and help visitors find the houses they are going to visit. They are also there so the gods that

---

上彩粉图案迎接客人。"彩粉图"意思是"颜色的混合"。这种图案是用大米粉制成的糨糊绘制的，糨糊一般是红色或黄色的。因为印度人认为红色和黄色能驱赶邪恶。一种传统的印度彩粉图案是荷花，是吉祥天女（印度教主神毗湿奴的妻子）的象征。

在排灯节期间，灯当然是最重要的。在节日前几周，制陶工就制作出了陶瓷的灯，即排灯。排灯节的第一天，每家都会买盏新灯，象征着新的开端。大街上到处都是灯，即使在没有电的地区也能看见几千盏陶瓷灯。这些灯迎接旅行者并帮助他们找到想参观的房屋，还有一个作用就是让神

---

lotus *n.* 荷花   symbolize *v.* 象征

people are remembering will see the lights and pay them a visit. In addition to light, there is noise—the noise of firecrackers. Families spend a lot of money on firecrackers and light them for four or five hours at night in their backyards and gardens. At the end of Diwali, there are also big fireworks displays that light up the sky.

Hindus start every day of Diwali by taking a bath. After their baths, family members will rub scented oils into each other's hair. Then they get dressed in new clothes for the festival. Women will wear lots of jewelry and may draw special patterns on their hands and feet with henna. Then they pray at the family *shrine*. Every Hindu home has a shrine with pictures and statues of different gods. The shrine is usually in the living room of the house, where it is easy to get together every day and pray. After they pray at the shrine, they go out and visit family, friends, and business *colleagues*. They take

---

能看到灯光并来拜访他们。除了光之外，还有鞭炮的声音。人们买来许多鞭炮，通常会在花园和后院燃放四五个小时。排灯节快结束时，还会燃放烟花，这能把整个天空照得通亮。

排灯节期间，人们都会用沐浴的方式来迎接新一天的开始，沐浴后，家庭成员之间还会相互在对方的头发上抹香油，然后穿上新衣服。妇女会佩带很多首饰，并在手和脚上用染剂画上特别的图案。然后，他们还要在家族圣坛上祈祷。印度每家都有座圣坛，上面有很多图画和神像。圣坛通常放在客厅，一家人聚在一起祈祷很方便。祈祷后，他们便出门去拜访亲朋好友或同事，给他们送去蜡烛和干果。他们相信送去甜蜜的东西，人们

---

shrine *n.* 圣坛；圣地　　　　　colleague *n.* 同事；同僚

gifts with them of candies and dry fruits. They believe if you give sweet things, people will think sweet things about you. Some people may go to the market where there are stalls selling sweets, flowers, and jewelry. There's also village dancing, and everyone can join in. At the end of the day, they all go home to eat and light *fireworks*.

Diwali is a time when people look forward to good luck and wealth in the year to come. The Hindu goddess of wealth, Lakshmi, is honored during the festival. People hope that a visit from this goddess will bring them good luck. To help Lakshmi enter their homes, they leave all the windows and doors open and make sure there are lights shining at every door and window so that she can find her way in easily. Businesspeople put out all their account books for Lakshmi to *inspect*. Hindus pay their bills and leave money and jewelry on the shrine to her in their house.

就会认为你懂得生活的甜蜜。也有人去市场，那里有很多糖果、鲜花和珠宝的摊点。还有很多村庄舞蹈，每个人都可以加入。傍晚，他们就回家吃饭，放烟花。

人们通过排灯节来祈求来年的好运和财富。在节日期间，主要纪念印度的财神——吉祥天女。人们希望她的拜访能带来好运。为了方便吉祥天女的拜访，人们把所有的门窗都打开，点灯照亮每个角落以使她能很快找到来路。商人也拿出账簿供吉祥天女审阅。印度人结完账后把剩余的现金和珠宝放在圣坛上留给她。

---

firework *n.* 烟火

inspect *v.* 检查；审查

In western India, Diwali starts the new business year. There is a ceremony of closing the account books and showing them to Lakshmi. Businesspeople who *take part in* the ceremony have red marks on their foreheads. During Diwali, people always visit their coworkers and send "Happy Diwali" cards and exchange gifts.

Hindus in other parts of the world also celebrate Diwali. Outside India, the temple is more important in the festivities than the home is. This is because Diwali is not a long public holiday in other countries, and Hindus have to go to work as usual. The temple is a good place for them to meet for the festivities. Outside India, Hindus usually spend their whole day in the temple, whereas in India they would go there to *pray* to the gods and then go home. In the temple during Diwali, the priests dress the figures of the gods in brightly colored silk clothes to receive their visitors. When visitors come, they ring

在印度西部，排灯节是新的财政年度的开端，这时会举行仪式，把账簿合上给吉祥天女审阅，每个参加仪式的商人前额上都有红色的标记。节日期间，人们会走亲访友，互送"排灯节"贺卡，交换礼物。

其他国家的印度人也会庆祝排灯节。对他们来说，寺庙远比家重要。因为在其他国家，排灯节不是公众假期，他们也得像平常那样工作。寺庙是他们在节日期间聚会的好去处。虽然印度人通常去寺庙祈祷完后就回家，但其他国家的印度人一整天都呆在寺庙。这期间的寺庙，僧侣们给神像穿上色彩鲜艳的丝绸衣服来迎接客人。有拜访者时，他们就按铃告诉神

take part in 参与；参加　　　　　　　　　　　　　pray v. 祈祷

the temple bell to let the gods know that they have arrived, and they bring gifts of sweets and flowers. The temple is usually covered with offerings of sweets, flowers, fruit, and cakes. People bring food not only for the gods but also for themselves. Everybody eats and listens to traditional music. There are no *formal* religious services, but every visitor says a private prayer to the gods and asks for good fortune.

Diwali is a time to be happy and enjoy family and friends. It's a time when people exchange sweets, wear their new clothes, buy jewelry, and have a festive time. However, for the Hindus, Diwali is more than eating and shopping. Its burning lamp is a message of peace and *harmony* to the world.

灵有人来访，他们还会带来糖果和鲜花等礼物。寺庙里几乎到处都是糖果、鲜花、蛋糕等供品。人们带来的食物不仅供神，自己也吃。他们一边吃一边欣赏传统音乐。虽然没有正式的宗教仪式，每个人都会向神许愿祈求好运。

排灯节是个快乐的节日，家人和朋友可以欢聚一堂。人们互送糖果，穿新衣服，买首饰，共享美好时光。但是对印度人来说，排灯节不只是吃喝、购物，点燃的灯还给世界带来和平、和谐的信号。

---

formal *adj.* 正式的   harmony *n.* 和谐；融洽

15

What Is the Story Behind the 1,001 Arabian Nights?

The 1,001 *Arabian Nights*, also known as *The Book of One Thousand and One Nights*, is one of the most famous pieces of Arabic literature. It includes many well-known stories, such as *Ali Baba and the Forty Thieves*, *Sinbad the Sailor*, and *Aladdin's Lamp*. In all, the *collection* of stories contains about

《一千零一夜》背后的故事

《一千零一个阿拉伯夜晚》即俗称的《一千零一夜》是阿拉伯国家最有名的文学名著之一，它包括许多家喻户晓的故事，如《阿里巴巴与四十大盗》，《辛巴达历险记》，《阿拉丁神灯》。总之，它从阿拉伯、印度、波斯（今伊朗）甚至中国收集了大约

collection *n.* 收集；采集

200 folk tales from Arabia, India, Persia(modern day Iran), and even China. Many people in these countries shared a religion, Islam, and the Arabic language of the Koran.

These stories are very ancient and are believed to first have been told by an Arab storyteller in the ninth century. There are various types of stories: love stories, historical tales, comedies, tragedies, poems, and religious legends. The stories *depict* what life was like at the time and include good and bad rulers, magicians, and lots of *adventure*. The stories have been told and retold for generations. Later on, in the Middle Ages, a "frame" to all these stories was added. The frame for the large group of stories is the story of Sherezade. In her tale, she tells many of *The 1,001 Arabian Nights stories*.

The story of Sherezade begins with the tale of a king named Shahryar who rules an unnamed island"between India and China".

二百个民间故事。这些国家的许多人都信仰伊斯兰教，讲阿拉伯语。

这些故事非常久远，有人说最初是公元9世纪一个专门讲故事的阿拉伯人讲的。故事分很多种：爱情故事、历史故事、喜剧、悲剧、诗歌和宗教传说。这些故事讲述了当时人们的生活状况，包括英明或昏庸的统治者、魔术师和许多冒险故事。故事被一代一代地传下去。后来到中世纪，又有许多故事加了进去，故事的主体围绕雪瑞萨德展开，讲了她许多故事。

雪瑞萨德的故事是从一个叫沙赫瑞亚尔的国王开始的，他统治着印度中部一个不知名的岛屿。他爱他的妻子胜过一切，对她非常忠诚，并愿意

---

depict *v.* 描述；描写　　　　　　　　　　adventure *n.* 冒险

Shahryar had a wife whom he loved more than anything in the world. He was devoted to her and would do anything for her. However, after several years, he discovered completely by accident that she had been unfaithful to him. *Betrayed*, the King carried out the law of the land and ordered his chief minister to put her to death. Then the heartbroken king went out of his mind and declared that all women were unfaithful like his wife. The fewer there were of them, he thought, the better the world would be. So every evening he married a new wife and commanded that she be *executed* the following morning.

It was job of the chief minister to provide the king with these unfortunate brides. The chief minister did his duty with great *reluctance*, for it was hard for him to see a woman married one day and then killed the next. The people of the town lived in sadness and fear. Fathers and mothers cried about the fate of their daughters. The

---

为她付出一切。但几年后偶然发现她背叛了他，于是他下令把她处死。被出卖之后，伤心欲绝的国王变得很疯狂，他认为所有的妇女都像他妻子那样不忠贞，认为妇女越少，世界就会越美好。于是他每天晚上都会娶一位妻子，并于第二天早上把她处死。

　　负责把不幸的新娘送给国王的是首席大臣，他非常不愿意做这件事，因为实在不忍心看着女人第一天结婚，第二天就被处死。那个小镇的人都生活在悲伤和恐惧中，父母为女儿的命运哭泣不已。首席大臣自己也有两

---

betray *v.* 出卖；背叛　　　　　　　　　　　execute *v.* 处死
reluctance *n.* 不愿；勉强

chief minister himself had two daughters: Sherezade and Dinarzade. Sherezade was older; she was a clever and brave girl. Her father had given her the best education, and she was one of the most beautiful girls in the kingdom.

One day, Sherezade asked her father a favor. Her father loved her very much, and he would not refuse her anything that was reasonable. Sherezade then told him that she was determined to end the cruel practice of the king. She had a plan to save the women of the kingdom from their terrible fate. Since her father had to provide the king with a new wife every day, she *implored* him to choose her. Her father was shocked by her request and thought she had *lost* her *senses*. But Sherezade explained that if her plan succeeded, she would do a great service for her country. After she begged and begged him, her father finally agreed to Sherezade's wish. He went to the palace to tell the king that the following evening he would

---

个女儿：雪瑞萨德和迪纳萨德。大女儿雪瑞萨德是个聪明勇敢的女孩，她父亲给了她最好的教育，她也是王国里最漂亮的女孩之一。

有一天，雪瑞萨德向他父亲提出请求。他父亲非常爱她，只要是合理的要求从来不会拒绝。她想让国王停止这种残暴行为，并有办法解救这些可怜的女人。由于是她父亲负责挑选新娘，她希望父亲能让自己去。她父亲听后很震惊，还以为她疯了。雪瑞萨德解释，如果她的计划成功，就为国家做了件大好事。经过再三的央求，她父亲最终同意了。他去王宫告诉国王那晚将由他的女儿来做新娘，国王也很吃惊，问他为何牺牲自己的女

---

implore v. 恳求；哀求

lose sense 失去理智

bring him Sherezade to be the new queen. The *astonished* king asked him why he would sacrifice his own daughter. The chief minister replied that it was her wish. The king then told the minister to bring his daughter to the palace.

When her father returned to tell her, Sherezade was happy and thanked her father for agreeing to her wish. She then went to prepare herself for the marriage. But, first, she wanted to speak with her sister, Dinarzade. Sherezade told her sister that she had a plan and needed her help. She said her father was going to take her to the palace to celebrate her marriage with the king. As a final wish, she would ask the king to let her sister sleep in their bedroom during the last night that she was alive. If the king *granted* her wish, which she hoped he would, then Dinarzade should wake her up an hour before daybreak and say these words to her, "My sister, if you are not asleep, please tell me one of your charming stories." Then

---

儿，首席大臣说这是他女儿自己的意愿。国王便让他把女儿带过来。

父亲回到家告诉雪瑞萨德后，她非常高兴，还对他父亲满足了她的愿望表示感谢。于是，她开始准备出嫁了。但首先她想和妹妹迪纳萨德谈话，告诉妹妹自己的计划，并希望能得到她的协助。她告诉妹妹父亲要带她去宫殿和国王举行婚礼，作为最后一个愿望，她会要求国王允许妹妹来宫殿陪自己度过最后一个夜晚，如果国王同意（她觉得国王会同意的），妹妹就在天亮前一个小时叫醒她，并说："姐姐，如果你睡不着，就给我讲个有趣的故事吧。"然后，她就开始讲故事，希望通过这个办法解救人

---

astonished *adj.* 感到震惊的　　　　　　　　grant *v.* 允许；同意

Sherezade would begin to tell a tale, and she hoped by this to save the people from their terrible fate. Dinarzade said she would do what her sister asked of her.

When the time for the marriage came, the chief minister took Sherezade to the *palace* and left her alone with the king. The king told her to raise her veil and was amazed at her beauty. But Sherezade had tears in her eyes. When the king asked what was the matter, Sherezade said that she had a sister whom she loved very much, and she asked the king if he would allow her sister to spend the night in the same room since it would be the last time they would be together. The king agreed to her wish.

An hour before daybreak, Dinarzade *woke up* and asked Sherezade,"My sister, if you are not asleep, please tell me one of your charming stories before the sun rises. It is the last time I'll have

---

们。妹妹答应了她的所有要求。

　　婚礼要开始时，首席大臣把雪瑞萨德带进了皇宫，并把她和国王单独留在一起。国王让她揭开面纱后一下子被她的美貌惊呆了。但雪瑞萨德眼里含泪，国王问及原因时，她说她有个深爱的妹妹，希望国王能允许她们最后一个夜晚在同一房间过夜，国王答应了她的要求。

　　离天亮还有一个小时，迪纳萨德醒来对她姐姐说：“姐姐，如果你睡不着，就在天亮前给我讲个有趣的故事吧，这是最后一次了。”雪瑞萨德问国王可否答应她妹妹的要求，“当然”，国王同意了，于是她开始讲故

---

palace *n.* 宫殿　　　　　　　　　　　　　　　wake up 醒来；起床

the pleasure of hearing you." Sherezade asked the king if he would let her do as her sister requested. "Of course," answered the king. So Sherezade began to tell the king a story. But when she reached the most exciting part of it, she stopped. She said that if he wanted to hear the end he would have to let her live another day. Each night she would tell him a story, ending at daybreak with a "cliff hanger" — leaving off at an exciting part.

The enchanted king always wanted to hear the rest of the story, and so he *put off* her death night after night. He was dazzled by her thrilling stories, and soon he fell in love with her. Sherezade was able to *spin* a new tale for 1,001 nights. By this time, she had given birth to three sons, and the king became convinced of her faithfulness. Sherezade's plan was successful, and all the people rejoiced because the women in the kingdom were saved.

事，讲到高潮时就停下了。她对国王说如果想知道结果就必须让她再活一天。就这样，她每天晚上都讲个吊人胃口的故事，快天亮时就停止——只剩下精彩的结尾。

着了迷的国王总想听到故事的结尾，所以他无限期地推迟了雪瑞萨德的死期。他被她精彩的故事深深地吸引住了，并渐渐地爱上了她。雪瑞萨德每晚都能编出个故事，这样过了一千零一个夜晚。在这期间，她生了三个儿子，令国王完全相信了她的忠诚。这样，她的计划大功告成，全国人民都因该国的女人获救而兴奋不已。

---

put off 推迟；推后　　　　　　　　　　　　　spin　*v.* 编造；撰写

Who Were the Samurai?

The samurai were warriors, or fearless soldiers, who became powerful in Japan around the 1200s. The samurai, which means "those who serve", were hired by lords to fight their wars and protect their land. The samurai were expert fighters; they were skilled with the sword and the bow and arrow, and they were superior horsemen. They were athletic and strong, and they developed their fighting skills into what is the basis of modern martial arts.

The samurai had a code of *ethics* called Bushido, which meant

何谓日本武士？

日本武士即战士，是英勇的士兵，是在公元1200年左右发展起来的。"武士"在日语中的意思是"服务的人"。他们被地主雇佣来打仗和保卫领地。他们英勇善战，对剑、弓和箭的运用得心应手，马术也相当不错。他们体格健壮，所掌握的攻击技巧是当代武术的基础。

日本武士有一套道德标准，即所谓的"武士道"精神，意思是"武士

---

ethic *n.* 道德；行为准则

"way of the warrior." The samurai had to have unquestionable *loyalty* to the emperor and their lord (the daimyo). They were trustworthy, honest, and kind and generous to the poor. They led *frugal* lives and had no interest in wealth or material things. They were only interested in honor and pride. Additionally, they had to be men of noble spirit who were not afraid to die, because death in battle only meant honor to their lord and family. If samurai lost a battle or a fight, they would have to commit suicide rather than face dishonor.

The samurai developed a special way of dressing. They wore their hair tied back in a top-knot, and their brow and crown were shaved. Samurai wore simple clothes when they were not fighting. However, when they were fighting they wore a suit of armor that

---

的行为准则"。日本武士对天皇和地主们绝对忠诚。他们可信赖、诚实、善良，对穷人也非常慷慨。他们生活很节俭，对财富或物质享受没有什么兴趣，只对荣誉感兴趣。此外，他们必须具有男人的高贵品质，即不怕死。因为战死沙场是地主和家族的荣誉。日本武士如果在战斗中被击败，他们宁愿自杀也不愿面对屈辱。

日本武士的着装很特别，他们把头发卷起来打成结。前额和头顶都剃得很干净。他们平时着装很简朴；但战时则身披用皮革或铁条做成的盔

---

loyalty *n.* 忠诚；忠心　　　　　frugal *adj.* 节俭的；朴素的

was made from leather or iron strips so it was completely *flexible*. Their most important weapon and sign of their class was a pair of matching swords. Only samurai had the right to carry swords. They believed that swords had special powers. The people who made swords were master *craftsmen*, and to this day people can tell who created the sword of a samurai by the way the blade was made.

The wives of the samurai followed the same code of ethics as the men did. Since the *privileges* and rights of the samurai were passed down from father to son, it was important for a wife to have a male child. Sometimes a samurai took another wife if the first wife did not give birth to a son. Samurai women were trained fighters like their husbands. They kept a short knife in a piece of silk material they wrapped around their waist. They also were trained to use long, curved swords. In times of war, they fought to defend their homes

---

甲，活动起来非常方便。只有武士才有权佩剑，他们认为剑有特殊的力量。制剑人都是工匠能手，到今天，人们也能从剑锋的形状分辨出制剑人。

日本武士的妻子也遵循这种道德准则。由于武士的特权可以由父亲传给儿子，所以有个儿子对妻子来说非常重要。有时，如果第一个妻子不能生儿子，他们会再娶。妻子们也像丈夫一样被训练成战士。她们腰间总有一把丝绸布包起来的短刀。另外，她们也受训使用长而弯的剑。战时，她们保卫家园，有时还与男人们同场作战。

---

flexible *adj.* 灵活的　　　　　　　　　　craftsman *n.* 工匠；手艺人
privilege *n.* 特权

and sometimes joined the men in battle.

In the beginning, samurai women were very independent. However, after the 1600s, they had to follow the religious beliefs of that time. These beliefs included the teachings of the "Three *Obediences*." This stated that a woman had no independence through life. When she was young, she obeyed her father; when she married, she obeyed her husband; when she was widowed, she obeyed her son. Samurai women are remembered as being courageous, no matter what they suffered. Today, a play is still performed in Japan about two brave samurai sisters who fought to avenge their father's death.

Until the 1600s, the samurai belonged to a special class of people that fought and farmed the land they lived on. However, during the Edo period (1600-1867), their *status* and way of life

---

最初，这些妇女非常独立，但是，到了17世纪后，他们就开始遵从当时的宗教信仰，这些信仰包括"三从"的说教，这样一来，妇女的一生就没有自由了：小时得听父亲的，结婚后得听丈夫的，成寡妇又得听儿子的。这些妇女不管遭受什么困难都特别英勇。有一部戏剧至今仍在日本上演，讲述的是两姐妹为父亲报仇雪恨英勇奋战的故事。

在17世纪以前，日本武士都属于一个特殊的阶层，他们在自己的土地上作战、耕作。但是，到了江户时期，他们的地位和生活方式发生了变

---

obedience *n.* 顺从；服从   status *n.* 地位

changed. Japan had become a peaceful country, and its rulers didn't want the samurai to fight anymore. They made the samurai live permanently in castles, paid them with rice, and gave them many special rights. Though some samurai worked for the government, many others lived the relaxed life of the upper class. During this time, some samurai helped create the forms of art that we consider to be typically Japanese. These include haiku poetry, the No style of drama, the tea *ceremony*, and flower arranging.

Around 1867, the leadership and government changed in Japan. The emperor once again became the ruler of the country. The lords were ordered to give their land to the emperor, and in return they received money from the state. In 1871, the samurai class was *abolished*. The samurai had lost their land and status; some did not know how to survive.

化。日本成为爱好和平的国家，统治者不希望武士再作战。他们让武士永远住在城堡，给他们提供食物，赋予他们特殊的权利。尽管有些武士仍为政府工作，但大多数还是过着上层人的愉快生活。他们利用这段时间创作了许多日本特有的艺术，包括俳句诗、无特殊形式的戏剧、茶道和插花。

1867年左右，日本的领导阶层发生了变化。天皇又一次成了国家的统治者。地主的土地必须上交天皇。作为回报，政府付给他们金钱。1871年，武士制度被废除，他们失去了土地和地位，有的人根本不知道如何生存。

1877年，一些不满的武士联合起来与天皇对抗。尽管保持对天皇的忠

---

ceremony *n.* 礼节；礼仪　　　　　　　　　　abolish *v.* 废止；废除

In 1877, some of the unhappy samurai formed a group to fight the emperor. Even though loyalty to the emperor was the highest of samurai values, these warriors felt that they had to fight in order to protect their culture and the future of all samurai people. A samurai called Saigo Takamori led twenty thousand samurai *rebels* against sixty thousand government soldiers. The government had a modern army with modern weapons. The samurai were brave fighters, but their weapons were *inferior*. They lost battle after battle, and finally Saigo and his remaining group went into the hills. They knew they had no chance; nevertheless, they fought to the end. Saigo was wounded and committed suicide in the samurai tradition. Later, Saigo Takamori, now known as "the last samurai", became a hero for the Japanese. Today, the descendants of the samurai have high *esteem* among the Japanese, although they have no official status.

诚是他们至高无上的荣誉，但为了保护他们的文化和将来，他们不得不与天皇对抗。一个叫西乡隆盛的武士带领两万反抗者对抗六万政府士兵。政府领导的军队有现代化的装备，虽然武士很英勇，但他们的武器太落后，每次作战都以失败告终，最后他带领残兵败将回到山里。尽管他们知道胜利的希望很渺茫，但他们仍然坚持战到最后。最后，西乡隆盛负伤，他按照武士的习惯自杀了。后来，他被称为"最后的武士"，被日本人尊为英雄。现在，在日本，武士的后代虽然没有官位，但一直颇受人们的尊敬。

尽管武士时代后日本政府和社会发生了许多变化，但格斗思想都以不

---

rebel *v.* 反抗   inferior *adj.* 下等的；差的
esteem *n.* 敬重

Although the Japanese government and society have gone through many changes since the time of the samurai, Bushido values have continued in different forms. After World War II, Japan no longer had an army. It became a modern, *industrialized* country with huge companies. These companies were like families, and loyalty to one's company and company name was important. Even today, workers for these companies have great respect for their bosses. They do not want to do anything wrong that would bring shame to their company, themselves, or their family. Such loyalty and respect for country, leaders, and family is one example of the continuing influence of the great samurai warriors on Japanese society. Though the samurai culture has *disappeared*, important parts of it live on in this way.

同形式存在着。二战后，日本不再保留军队，成为一个现代化的拥有许多大型公司的工业国。那些公司就像家族一样。对公司和公司名誉的忠诚是至关重要的。即使在今天，公司的员工对老板也特别尊敬，他们不会做任何有损公司形象，有损自己形象或家庭利益的事，这种对国家，上司和家族的忠诚和尊敬是伟大的武士道精神一直延续的典型表现。尽管武士文化消失了，但它的精髓仍然以这种方式存活着。

---

industrialized *adj.* 工业化的   disappear *v.* 消失；不复存在

17

How Did Chopsticks Originate?

In the beginning, people used just their fingers to eat. Then came the finger-and-knife combination. Around 5,000 years ago, while the rest of the world was still using fingers and a knife, the Chinese began using *chopsticks*. Today many people eat with a combination of knives, spoons, and forks, but chopsticks are still as important and popular as they were centuries ago.

No one knows exactly when the Chinese began to use chopsticks. According to one Chinese legend, the use of chopsticks

筷子的起源

最初，人们是用手抓饭吃的，后来又加上餐刀。大约五千年前，当世界其他地方的人们仍在使用餐刀时，中国人就开始使用筷子了。当今人们不仅用餐刀，还用羹和叉子，但筷子仍像几个世纪前那样重要和受欢迎。

没有人确切地知道中国人是何时开始使用筷子的。根据民间传说，筷子的使用源于两个被逐出村庄的农民。他们走遍了所有的村庄都非常不

chopstick *n.* 筷子

began when two poor farmers were thrown out of their village. The farmers went from village to village, but were not welcome anywhere. The two men grew tired and hungry, so they stole a piece of meat from a storeroom in a small village. Then they ran from the village and into a forest, where they quickly made a fire to cook their meat. The smell of the roasting meat was so good that the two men could not wait any longer. Using some sticks from the forest floor, they took the pieces of meat from the fire and put them into their mouths. And so began the popularity of chopsticks. Other people did the same, and in a short time people all over China were eating with chopsticks.

There are other ideas about why the Chinese started using chopsticks. Some people believe that the *philosopher* Confucius influenced how the Chinese thought about many things, including how they ate. Confucius, a vegetarian, said it was wrong to have knives at the table because knives were used for killing. Another idea is that there was not enough *fuel* in China. There was only a small

---

受欢迎，他们又累又饿，就从一个小村庄的库房里偷了块肉，然后跑出村庄奔向森林，迅速生火烤肉。烤肉的香味扑鼻而来，他们迫不及待地想尝尝，于是就在地上随手捡了几根棍子夹肉吃。筷子就这样开始流行起来，其他人也开始效仿，在很短时间内，全中国人都开始使用筷子了。

对于中国人为何使用筷子还有很多说法。许多人认为中国人思考问题的方法包括就餐的方式深受哲学家孔子的影响。孔子是个素食主义者，他认为在餐桌上使用刀具是不对的，因为刀是用来杀生的。另一种说法就是当时

---

philosopher *n.* 哲学家

fuel *n.* 燃料

amount of fuel available for the cooking of food. But the Chinese found the *solution* !They cut up the food into small pieces before cooking, so it would cook as quickly as possible and only use a very small amount of fuel. The small pieces of food were well suited for chopsticks. It is not certain which came first: chopsticks or the unique style of Chinese cooking. But it is certain that chopsticks did have a great influence on the development of Chinese cooking.

Chopsticks spread from China to Vietnam and Korea and eventually reached Japan by the year 500. Over 3,000 years and between different cultures, several *variations* of chopsticks developed. Chinese chopsticks are nine to ten inches long and round or square at the top end. The Vietnamese did not change the Chinese chopsticks, but the Koreans made their chopsticks a little thinner and then started to make them from metal. Korea is the only country today that uses metal chopsticks. The Japanese made

---

中国没有足够的燃料，能供烹饪的燃料很少。但中国人找到了解决的办法。在烹饪之前，他们把食物切成小块，这样，不仅烹饪速度快，而且燃料消耗少。小块的食物非常适宜用筷子。但筷子和中国独特的烹饪方式究竟谁先谁后，我们已无从考证。但筷子确实对中国的烹饪发展产生过巨大的影响。

早在公元前五百年，筷子已经由中国传到越南、朝鲜，后来到了日本。三千年来，由于不同文化的碰撞，筷子也出现了不同的款式。中国的筷子有九到十英寸长，顶端是圆形或正方形。越南人保留了筷子的原样，但朝鲜人把筷子削薄了，还把金属作为原材料。当今只有朝鲜人才使用金属筷子。日本人把筷子做成圆的或尖的，比中国的筷子更短些——女性用

---

solution *n.* 解决办法

variation *n.* 变化

their chopsticks rounded and pointed. They are also shorter—seven inches long for females and eight inches long for males.

Every kind of material is used to make chopsticks. The vast majority of chopsticks are made from bamboo. Bamboo is cheap, heat resistant, and has no taste or *odor*. The wealthy have had chopsticks made from gold, *jade*, ivory, and silver. Some people had strong feelings about some of these materials. In fact, people once believed silver chopsticks would turn black if they touched any poison. An emperor who was afraid of being poisoned made his servants test each of the dishes with silver chopsticks before he ate. The emperor himself would not use silver chopsticks to eat; he thought the metal in his mouth was unpleasant. Today we know that silver doesn't react to poisons, but if bad eggs, onions, or garlic are used, the chemicals might change the color of silver chopsticks.

The Japanese made chopsticks from every kind of tree. They even

---

的七英寸，男性用的八英寸。

很多材料都可用来制作筷子，但大多数都采用竹子。竹子便宜、防热而且没有味道。有钱人都使用黄金、玉、象牙、银做的筷子。有的人对这些材料有些害怕。事实上，人们曾经认为银筷子如果碰上有毒的食物就会变黑。有个国王怕被人下毒，在他进餐前会让仆人用银筷子品尝每道菜，但他自己从不使用银筷子，他觉得把金属放进嘴里很难受。现在我们知道银并不会对毒产生反应，但如果使用变质的鸡蛋、洋葱或大蒜，这些化学元素就会使银筷子变色。

日本人用不同种类的树制作筷子。在四百年前，他们甚至把一种发

---

odor *n.* 气味

jade *n.* 玉

started to put lacquer, a kind of shiny paint, on chopsticks about 400 years ago. The lacquered chopsticks of modern Japan have designs and are beautiful to look at. They are given as special gifts because they are not only beautiful, but *durable*. The layers of lacquer make them last forever. The Wajima Nuri area in Japan is famous for making chopsticks with between 75 and 120 separate layers of lacquer. These chopsticks are harder than metal and can cost up to $125 a pair.

In 1878, the Japanese were also the first to make *disposable* wooden chopsticks. The disposable chopstick started when a Japanese schoolteacher named Tadao Shimamoto had packed his lunch and brought it to school with him but had left behind his pair of chopsticks. Fortunately, his school was in an area of Japan famous for its wood. He explained his problem to one of the local men. The man gave him a piece of wood from which Tadao made a pair of chopsticks. Anyone who has eaten in a Japanese or Chinese restaurant knows what these

---

光的涂料即油漆涂在筷子上。当今，日本涂了油漆的筷子上都有不同的图案，看起来非常美观，而且耐用，所以被视为特别的礼物，油漆层让它们经久耐用。日本的传统漆器制作中心就以制作75到120层漆的筷子而闻名全国。这些筷子比金属重，一般卖到125美元一双。

1878年，日本人开始使用一次性的木筷。这源于一个叫德岛的教师，他把午餐打包带到学校但忘了带筷子，幸好他工作的学校附近有大块的林地。他向当地人解释了他的情况后，那人给了他一块木头，他便做了双筷子。只要在中国或日本餐馆就过餐的人都知道这种筷子是什么样的。人们非常喜欢这种筷子。不久，当地人便开始大批量生产这种一次性筷

---

durable *adj.* 持久的；耐用的   disposable *adj.* 一次性的

look like. People liked his chopsticks so much that soon the local area started to produce large numbers of disposable chopsticks called wari-bashi. We do not know if Tadao made any money from wari-bashi, but certainly his name is remembered. Each year representatives from disposable chopstick *manufacturers* go to Tadao's hometown and perform a ceremony in honor of the father of wari-bashi.

About one-half of disposable chopsticks are produced in Japan; the rest come from China, Indonesia, Korea, and the Philippines. Japan uses about 24 billion pairs of disposable chopsticks a year, which is a lot of wood. In fact, it is enough to build over 10,000 homes. Japan now is trying to *eliminate* them for environmental reasons. Today, increasing numbers of Japanese are trying to help the environment. They carry their own personal chopsticks to restaurants instead of using disposable ones. But no matter what kind of chopsticks people use, chopsticks are here to stay.

子，人们把它称作瓦日－巴氏。我们不知道德岛是否从瓦日－巴氏中挣了很多钱，但人们记住了他的名字。每年，生产一次性筷子的厂家代表都会去德岛的家乡举行庆祝仪式纪念瓦日－巴氏的发明者。

世界上大约有一半的一次性筷子产于日本，另一半产于中国、朝鲜和菲律宾。日本每年消费二千四百万双筷子，消耗了大量的木材。这些木材至少可用来修建一万座房屋。现在出于环保的原因日本人决定不再使用一次性筷子了。如今越来越多的日本人参与环保，他们去饭店时自带餐具，不再使用一次性筷子了。但不管人们使用何种类型的筷子，筷子仍然存在着。

---

manufacturer　*n.*　制造商　　　　　　　　　　　　eliminate　*v.*　排除；消除

18

Why Do People Want to Climb Mount Everest?

When asked why he wanted to climb Mount Everest, the famous words of the British climber George Mallory were, "Because it is there." *Unfortunately*, to this day we do not know if George Mallory and his partner Andrew Irvine made it to the top when they tried to climb Everest

为什么要攀登珠峰？

当问及为何会攀登珠峰时，英国登山家乔治·马洛里回答"因为珠峰在那里"被誉为经典名言。遗憾的是，到目前为止，我们仍不清楚马洛里和他的同伴安德鲁·欧文是否到达了峰顶，因为他们在1924年的登峰的尝试中失去了生命。直到1999年，人们才在山上发现他们的尸体。对于马洛里和欧文的失踪，人们非常悲痛，珠峰神奇的名声也

---

unfortunately *adv.* 不幸地

in 1924. They died in the attempt, and it was only recently — in
1999 — that Mallory's body was found on the mountain. People were
sad about Mallory and Irvine's disappearance, and that is when the
fascination with Everest began. There are many reasons why people
climb mountains, such as personal satisfaction, *prestige*, power, the
difficulty, and the risk, but they may also do it to understand their
inner strength. The first man known to have climbed a mountain for
no reason other than it was there was Frenchman Antoine de Ville. In
1492, he climbed a mountain in France (Mont Aiguille) and liked the
view so much that he stayed there for six days.

Mount Everest, the highest mountain in the world, was named
after Sir George Everest, a British surveyor in India who recorded
the mountain's *location* in 1841. Mount Everest is in the Himalaya
Mountains in Nepal. Its official height, which was determined using
a Global Positioning System satellite in 1999, is 29,035 feet(8,850
meters). Until then, every time surveyors measured the mountain

---

就是从这时开始的。人们攀登珠峰有很多原因。比如个人满足感、名誉、
权力、困难和冒险，还可能是想了解内心的力量。第一个出于"因为珠峰在
那里"的原因而去登山的是法国人安东尼。1492年，他登上了法国的阿格尔
山，被山顶迷人的风景所深深吸引。他在山顶逗留了6天。

珠峰是世界上最高的山峰，是根据一个名叫乔治·埃菲勒斯的人命名
的，他是一名英国调查员，1841年他在印度记录下珠峰的地理位置。珠峰
位于尼泊尔的喜马拉雅山脉，1999年利用全球定位系统测出它的高度为
8850米。在这之前，每次调查员测出的数据都有出入，后来人们才明

---

prestige *n.* 声望；威望   location *n.* 位置

there was a difference of several feet. It was later found that the changing depth of ice at the *summit*, and not a mistake of the surveyors, was altering the mountain's height.

Many people had tried to climb Everest, but none were successful until 1953, when Edmund Hillary(later Sir Edmund Hillary) and Tenzing Norgay reached its summit. Edmund Hillary was from New Zealand, and Tenzing Norgay was a native Sherpa from Nepal. The Sherpas are skilled mountain climbers, and many of them are today's guides and porters in the expeditions to Everest.

Since 1953, many Everest records have been set by climbers who have tried the unprecedented. Ed Viesturs reached the summit without using extra *oxygen*. Junko Tabei was the first woman to reach the summit, and Lydia Bradley was the first woman to reach it without using extra oxygen. People with *disabilities* also have reached the mountaintop, such as a blind man, a man with one arm, and a

---

白，这并不是调查员测量的失误，是峰顶冰块不稳定的高度造成的。

许多人都尝试攀登珠峰。1953年埃德蒙·希拉里和藤辛·诺尔盖第一次成功到达峰顶。埃德蒙·希拉里是新西兰人，藤辛·诺尔盖是土生土长的尼泊尔雪巴人。雪巴人是登山能手，现在他们很多人都做登山者的导游和脚工。

从1953年起，许多登山者都打破了攀登珠峰的记录，他们都在尝试这种前所未有的创举。艾略·范恩没有用助氧器就到达了山顶，田部井淳子是第一名登上峰顶的女性，莉迪娅·布兰得利是第一个没用助氧器到达山顶的女性。残疾人同样能到达山顶，曾经有个盲人，一个只有一只胳膊和一条腿的人到达过峰顶。2003年，一个70岁的老人登上峰顶，是登顶

---

summit *n.* 顶点　　　　　　　　　　　oxygen *n.* 氧气
disability *n.* 残疾

man with one leg. In 2003, a seventy-year-old man became the oldest person to reach the summit. People have skied and snowboarded from the summit, three brothers reached it on the same day, and one person climbed Everest to sleep there. He slept for 21 hours! Speed records also have been set. The most recent one was 10 hours 56 minutes.

Needless to say, with all these attempts there have been many accidents and deaths on Everest. A blizzard in May 1996 killed eight climbers in one day. These climbers were in the best physical condition and had laptop computers, satellite phones, and other advanced *equipment* to help them climb the mountain. We know that sixty people died in the 1990s alone. In fact, one of every three climbers attempting to reach the summit has died, and yet climbers continue to risk their lives.

Today Everest has lost some of its old *mystique* and appeal because so many people are reaching its top. Thousands of

---

年纪最大的人。人们都会从峰顶滑雪或乘滑雪板下山。有三兄弟同一天到达峰顶，其中一个在那过夜，共睡了21个小时，打破了峰顶睡眠时间最长的纪录，最近的一次是10小时56分钟。

　　不用说，在这些成功的背后也有很多事故和死亡。1996年5月的一场暴风雪在一天内就夺去了8名登山者的生命。这些人体格都很健壮，还有手提电脑，卫星电话和其他先进的辅助设备。我们知道仅在20世纪90年代就有60人失去生命，事实上有三分之一的珠峰攀登者失去了生命，但人们还是会冒着生命危险去尝试。

　　如今有相当多的人曾到达山顶，所以珠峰就失去了原来的神秘感和

---

equipment　*n.* 设备；装备　　　　　　　mystique　*n.* 奥秘；神秘

mountaineers pass through base camp every year, but don't go as far as the summit. Close to 2,000 climbers have reached the summit, coming from every possible route. On May 16, 2002, fifty-four climbers reached the top successfully on the same day! These days, climbing Mount Everest has become a *novelty* for those who are in good physical condition and can *afford* to pay as much as $65,000 for climbing guides and fees. There are only a few months in the year that weather conditions make it practical to climb the mountain. These are April, May, October, December, and January. As a result, people usually have to make plans in advance to climb Everest. At one point, there was a twelve-year wait! It looks like the highest mountain in the world is becoming quite crowded. On the mountain, there is usually a line of people waiting their turn to get to the top. Even Sir Edmund Hillary is not pleased with the crowds. He said that if he were younger, he would not want to be in an expedition with so

魅力。每年有几千名登山者穿越营地，攀登珠峰，可真正能到达峰顶的却没有多少人。有将近两千人曾经由不同的路线攀登过珠峰。2002年5月16日，有54个登山者同时登上珠峰。在这个时期，攀登珠峰成了身体健康且能支付65,000美元导游费和登山费用的人们的时尚。由于气候原因，一年中只有几个月的时间允许登山，即4、5、10、12月和来年的1月。因此，人们在登山前须有很多准备。从某种意义上说，是需要等待几个月。世界上最高的山峰开始变得拥挤起来。在山顶上，人们通常排着长队轮流登上顶峰。就是希拉里也对拥挤的人群很厌烦，如果再年轻点，他肯定不会跟

novelty *n.* 新颖；新奇的事物　　　　　　afford *v.* 给予；提供

many people around.

Communication has always been a problem in such a remote area as Nepal. The nearest telephones from base camp, which is at 17,000 feet (5,182 meters), are a four-day walk away. These days, most trekkers (people who go on long and difficult walks) use satellite phones to run Web sites to contact their friends and family at home. Recently, someone had a better idea. A Sherpa, the grandson of a man from Nepal who was in the first expedition fifty years ago, plans to make an Internet café at the base camp of Everest. This will be the highest Internet café in the world! He is waiting for *permission* from the government to go ahead with the project. The money from the café will go to a project to clean up the tons of garbage left behind by the tens of thousands of tourists that come to Nepal every year.

这么多人一起探险。

在尼泊尔这个偏僻的地区，联系交流是个大问题。离营地最近的电话也有5182米远，近四天的路程。这些天，许多跋涉者（需要艰苦步行很长一段路的旅行者）都利用卫星电话和网络与家庭、朋友保持联系。最近，有人想出了更好的主意。他是50年前第一批探险到达峰顶的一个尼泊尔人的孙子，雪巴人，他计划在珠峰营地设网吧，这是世界上最高的网吧。他正等待政府的许可来执行自己的计划。网吧赚的钱全部捐助给一项清洁工程，这项工程是清扫每年来尼泊尔的几万游客留下的几吨垃圾。

---

communication *n.* 联络；联系   permission *n.* 允许；许可

Each of these tourists has his or her own reasons for climbing Everest. For many, the more challenging the mountain, the more they like it. These people know they risk their lives, but they don't mind. However, for many *extreme* climbers today, reaching the top of Mount Everest is not the challenge it once was, because too many people have done it. Many climbers want to go where no one has dared. Though it may be true that Mount Everest has lost some of its mystique, it is still the highest mountain on Earth. For this reason, it will probably always *attract* many of the world's best climbers.

这些游客都有各自登山的原因。对大多数人来说，山峰越有挑战性，他们越喜欢。尽管他们都知道那是有生命危险的，但他们并不在意。但是对今天许多极限登山者来说，登上珠峰已不像以前那样是个挑战，因为有太多人都曾到过峰顶。许多登山者都喜欢去别人不敢去的地方。尽管珠穆朗玛峰确实失去了一些神秘，但它仍然是地球上最高的山峰。也正因为如此，它才仍会吸引许多世界上最好的登山者。

extreme *adj.* 极度的；极端的   attract *v.* 吸引

Why Is Napoleon Famous?

Many portraits of Napoleon show him with his right hand placed inside his coat or shirt. In fact, there was nothing wrong with Napoleon's hand. At the time, portrait painters thought this *pose* made men look more *dignified*. Also, they had one less hand to draw and paint. Looking at his portraits, we can tell that Napoleon

拿破仑因何出名?

在许多关于拿破仑的画像里,他都是把右手放在外套或衬衣里。事实上,并不是他的手有问题。那时,画家认为这种姿势会使人看起来更尊贵些,另外他们也可以少画一只手。从他的画像中,我们可

pose *n.* 姿势;姿态　　　　　　　　dignified *adj.* 庄重的;有尊严的

was an important person. But who was this man?

Napoleon Bonaparte was born in 1769 on the French island of Corsica, not far from the coast of Italy. He was one of fourteen children. As a boy, Napoleon loved to play soldiers with his brothers. When he was old enough, his parents sent him to military school to learn how to become a real soldier. After he completed his training at the military school, Napoleon became an officer in the French army.

Four years later, in 1789, there was a sudden and violent change in France. Tired of paying heavy taxes so the king and his *nobles* could live in luxury, poor and middle-class people started a *revolution*. They executed the king and queen and many of their royal friends and then declared France a republic where all people were to pay taxes according to their wealth.

When the rulers of other European countries heard what happened in France, they thought they, too, would lose control

以看出他是个非常显要的人物。但这个人究竟是个什么样的人呢?

拿破仑·波拿巴于1769年出生在离意大利不远的法国科西嘉岛,家里兄弟姐妹共14个。作为男孩,他喜欢和兄弟们一起扮演士兵打仗。长到一定年龄后,父母就把他送到军事学校去学习如何做个真正的士兵。在军校完成学业后,他加入法国军队,成为一名军官。

四年后,也就是1789年,法国突然发生暴乱。国王和贵族为了过奢侈安逸的生活向穷人和中产阶级征收重税,使他们终于不堪重负起来反抗。他们处死了国王、王后和其他皇室成员,然后宣布法兰西为共和国,人们根据拥有财产的多少来纳税。

欧洲其他国家的君主得知在法国所发生的情况后,也开始担心会失去

noble *n.* 贵族   revolution *n.* 革命

over their countries. Austria and Britain went to war with the new republic of France. Napoleon was a brilliant officer and was only twenty-seven years old when he was made Commander-in-Chief of the French army in Italy. He won one victory after another, *defeating* the Austrians in eighteen battles. Then he moved his army to Egypt to stop the British trade route to India. He won a victory over the Egyptians in 1798 at the Battle of the Pyramids. In 1799, his troops in Egypt discovered the Rosetta stone, an important object which helped people to understand ancient Egyptian writing for the first time. Napoleon had with him *scholars* from many fields who wanted to set up schools in Egypt. One group of scholars studied the pyramids and started the science of Egyptology. However, the British destroyed Napoleon's ships and he lost the Rosetta stone to them. Then Napoleon decided to return to France.

对人民的控制。奥地利和英国联合起来对法国发动了战争。拿破仑是个非常出色的军官，在意大利被选为法军总司令时年仅27岁。他屡战屡胜，历经18场战役后打败了奥地利军队，之后，他指挥军队进驻埃及，阻断英国对印度的贸易航线。1798年，他赢得了金字塔战争的胜利，战胜了埃及人。1799年，他的军队在埃及境内发现了罗赛塔碑，这块碑帮助人们第一次了解到埃及文字。拿破仑把来自不同领域的想在埃及建立学校的学者组织起来，其中一批学者研究金字塔，开创了埃及考古学的先河。但是，英国人毁坏了拿破仑的船，夺走了罗赛塔石碑，于是拿破仑决定返回法国。

---

defeat *v.* 击败；战胜   scholar *n.* 学者

When Napoleon returned to France, he was appointed first consul. The French needed a strong ruler at this time, and Napoleon was one. He became consul for life in 1802, and in 1804, Napoleon declared himself emperor of France. The *Pope* came from Rome to perform the ceremony. Napoleon, richly dressed, listened to the service. Then Napoleon took the crown before the Pope could take it, and he put it on his own head. He did this to show that he got the crown because of his *wisdom* and military skill; he was not simply given the honor by the Pope.

Soon afterward, Napoleon made himself master of almost all of Europe. He *conquered* Austria in 1805 and Prussia in 1806. Then he formed an alliance with Russia, and he made one of his brothers the king of Spain and another brother king of Holland.

In France, he ruled wisely and well, and he restored law and

拿破仑回到法国后，被任命为第一执政官。那时法国正需要一个强有力的统治者，而拿破仑正是合适的人选。1802年，他被任命为终身第一执政官，1804年，他宣布自己为法兰西皇帝。罗马教皇专程从罗马赶来为他主持登基典礼。穿着异常雍容华贵的拿破仑聆听着教皇的说教，在教皇把皇冠递给他之前他就自己取来戴在头上。他这么做是为了向人们证明他的今天完全是靠他的智慧和军事才能换来的，而不是教皇给予的殊荣。

不久后，拿破仑成了整个欧洲的主人，1805年他征服奥地利，1806年征服普鲁士王国，接着与俄国结为联盟，他的两个兄弟也分别被他封为西班牙国王和荷兰国王。

他在法国的统治非常英明。革命后，他恢复了法律秩序，重组政府和

---

pope *n.* 教皇   wisdom *n.* 智慧；才智
conquer *v.* 征服

order after the revolution. He reorganized the French government and the Bank of France. He built many fine roads and improved the old ones. He turned Paris into a beautiful city with wide streets, fine bridges, and beautiful buildings and *monuments*, such as the Arc de Triomphe. More important still, he improved the laws. To this day, his *Napoleonic Code* is the foundation of European law, as well as of laws in Central and South America and Quebec in Canada. Napoleon wrote the Code's original 2,281 articles himself, although he was completely self-taught in legal matters. The Code created a legal system in which all citizens were equal. It was so clearly written that it could be read and understood by ordinary people at a time when all laws were written in Latin and understood by only a few.

Napoleon was a *genius* as an army commander. He conquered the huge Austrian Empire and ruled Italy, Switzerland, and Germany.

银行。他修建了许多新路还修补了许多废旧的路面。他把巴黎变成了拥有宽阔的街道，精美的桥梁，壮观的建筑和凯旋门这样纪念碑的美丽都市。更重要的是，他还改进了法律。直到今天，他的《拿破仑法典》仍是欧洲甚至中美，南美和加拿大的魁北克法律的基础。尽管他是自学的法律，但法典最初的2281个条款都是由他自己编写的。这套法典创建了一套合法的体系，在这个体系里，所有公民人人平等。那个时代，所有的法律都是用拉丁文写的，只有少数人能看懂，而这部法典的条文却写得非常清楚，连普通百姓也能读懂。

　　拿破仑是个军事天才，他征服了整个奥地利帝国，将意大利、瑞士和德国纳入自己的统治下。他组建了自古罗马时代以来最大的帝国。他唯

---

monument *n.* 纪念碑　　　　　　　　　　　　　　　　genius *n.* 天才

WHY IS NAPOLEON FAMOUS?

He had the largest empire seen in Europe since the days of the ancient Romans. The only country he could not defeat was Britain, losing to the British in 1805 in the Battle of Trafalgar. Then, in 1812, Napoleon made his biggest mistake by *invading* Russia. He entered Moscow, but he found that nearly all the people had left. There were fires all over the city, and most of it was destroyed. With no place to house his soldiers and no food for them to eat in the bitter Russian winter, Napoleon had no choice but to *retreat*. Napoleon lost half a million men in Russia. When he was finally defeated, he was sent to the island of Elba in the Mediterranean. By 1814, one million Frenchmen were dead. Napoleon was humiliated.

After ten months in Elba, Napoleon escaped, went back to France, and declared himself emperor again. He ruled for 100 days. In the meantime, the Europeans gathered their armies to end his

---

一征服不了的就是英国。在1805年特拉法加战争中，他输给了英国。在1812年，他又犯了致命的错误，那就是进攻俄国。当他攻进莫斯科后才发现那里已是人去楼空，整个城市一片火海，建筑物所剩无几。俄国的冬天非常严酷，他既没有地方驻扎士兵，也没有食物果腹，只好撤退。他在俄国损失了至少五十万士兵。当他最终被击败时，他已被驱逐到地中海一个叫厄尔巴的小岛上。到1814年，法国士兵损伤近一百万，他感到非常羞辱。

在被流放到厄尔巴岛10个月后，拿破仑逃回了法国，并再度称皇帝。这次他只统治了一百天，在这段时间里，欧洲集结兵力一举推翻了他

---

invade *v.* 侵略；侵入

retreat *v.* 撤退

rule. The combined armies, led by the British Duke of Wellington, defeated Napoleon at Waterloo in 1815. After this, he was sent to the island of St. Helena in the Atlantic Ocean, where he died six years later at age fifty-two. We do not know what Napoleon died of exactly. Some doctors argued that he died of *cancer*; others say he was poisoned.

Napoleon was a military genius and had a *brilliant* mind. He fought many wars and thought there would not be peace in Europe until the continent was under one ruler—himself. Perhaps Napoleon would have been an even greater ruler had he not been driven by his love of power.

的统治。由英国惠灵顿将军带领的联合军队于1815年在滑铁卢战场打败了拿破仑。此后，他被遣送到北大西洋的圣海伦娜岛。6年后死在那里，时年52岁。我们到现在也不知道他究竟是怎么死的。有些医生说他死于癌症，也有人说他中毒身亡。

拿破仑是个军事天才，他有着卓越的指挥才能，打了许多仗，认为欧洲大陆只有一个统治者，那就是他自己，否则那里的人们是不可能过上平静日子的。如果不是过于热衷权力，被权欲所驱动，他很可能会成为更加卓越的统治者。

---

cancer *n.* 癌症　　　　　　　　　　　brilliant *adj.* 聪颖的；杰出的

Who Invented the World Wide Web?

Tim Berners-Lee is not a household name like Bill Gates. He is not *outrageously* rich or famous. He could have been, but he didn't want to be. Tim Berners-Lee is a quiet man who does not like the *spotlight*. He is the man who invented the World Wide Web and revolutionized the Internet. Berners-Lee's

谁是万维网之父?

蒂姆·伯纳斯·李并不像比尔·盖茨那样家喻户晓,他可不是特别富有,也没有那么大的名气,他完全可以拥有这些,但他并不想这样。他是个很低调的人,不愿意成为媒体的焦点。他发明了万维网,革新了因特网。他的这项发明使任何拥有电脑的人都能轻易获得任何

---

outrageously *adv.* 无法容忍地   spotlight *n.* 媒体和公众的注意

invention permits anyone with a computer to easily access a vast amount of information on any subject. This is a great *contribution* to the use of computers and to society. Some people believe it is as important as Gutenberg's printing press.

Tim Berners-Lee was born in London, England, in 1955. He grew up in a family that talked a lot about computers and math, since both of his parents were computer scientists who worked on the design of the first commercial computer. As a small child, he made computers out of cardboard boxes. Later, when he attended Oxford University to study physics, he made his first real computer. He *constructed* it out of various parts of a machine and an old television set. He graduated from Oxford in 1976, and in the next few years worked for a few high-tech companies in England.

所需的信息。这对电脑的使用和社会的发展来说是一种巨大的贡献。有人认为它的重要性勘与古腾堡发明的活版印刷相媲美。

蒂姆·伯纳斯·李于1955年出生于英国伦敦，他的父母是电脑科学家，致力于第一代商业电脑的设计。他就是在这样一个经常谈论电脑和数学的家庭环境中长大的。孩提时，他用纸板箱制作电脑。后来，他在牛津大学学习物理，制作了第一台真正的电脑。他使用的原料是各种机器的零件和一台旧电视机。他于1976年毕业于牛津大学，在接下来的几年里，他都在英国的几个高科技公司工作。

---

contribution *n.* 贡献   construct *v.* 建造；构建

Around 1980, Berners-Lee was hired for a short period of time at the European Particle Physics Laboratory(CERN) in Geneva, Switzerland. It was there that he created a *software* program called Enquire that linked documents in the *laboratory*'s information system. The purpose of this system was to store a vast amount of information that could be accessed in a very short time span. This was the basis for the tool he later created and named the World Wide Web.

Berners-Lee left CERN to work for another computer company for a few years. When he returned, he found that his Enquire program had been forgotten. He suggested to his employer that Enquire could be expanded with graphics, text, and video to work on a worldwide basis using the Internet, which had been invented

---

1980年左右，他在瑞士日内瓦的欧洲粒子物理实验室工作，在这短暂的几个月里，他创立了微软"查询"信息处理工具，使实验室信息系统的文件能够共享。这个系统存储了大量可以在短时间内接触到的信息，这为他后来创造并命名的万维网奠定了基础。

不久，他离开了欧洲粒子物理实验室去了另外一家电脑公司工作了几年。回来时，他发现他的信息查询系统已被遗忘。他向老板建议信息查询系统可以通过图表、文本和影像的形式依靠因特网的支持扩展到全世界。而且他在1989年实现了这个想法。但欧洲粒子物理实验室没有能力开发

---

software *n.* 软件 laboratory *n.* 实验室

in 1989. But CERN was not a company that could *develop* such a project. So Berners-Lee worked on his own and created the World Wide Web.

Many people think that the World Wide Web and the Internet are the same thing, but they actually are not. The Internet is like a large bridge that connects millions of computers around the world and makes it possible for them to communicate with each other. There are different ways to send and receive information over the Internet. These include e-mail, *instant* messaging, and of course, the Web. Each of these ways uses a special set of rules that sends information over the bridge of the Internet.

The World Wide Web went on the Internet in 1991. In the beginning, it only had 600,000 users, mostly people in the

---

这个项目。因此，蒂姆·伯纳斯·李便独自一人创建了万维网联盟。

许多人认为万维网和因特网是一回事，但事实上并非如此。因特网就像一座大桥连接着世界上几百万台电脑，使他们能互相交流。通过因特网发送和接收信息有各种各样的方式，如电子邮件、即时讯息，当然还有万维网，这些途径都是用一套特殊的规则在因特网这座大桥上传输信息。

万维网于1991年在因特网上投入使用，最初只有60万用户，其中许

---

develop *v.* 开发；研制   instant *adj.* 立即的

educational field. But after a while, computer users understood the new *medium*. By 2002, it was estimated that some 600 million people worldwide were using the Web.

Undoubtedly, Berners-Lee must have turned down numerous offers with which he could have made a lot of money. But making money is not his goal. He is an *idealist* whose main pursuit is knowledge. In 1994, Berners-Lee joined the Laboratory for Computer Science at the Massachusetts Institute of Technology (M.I.T.). He has been working there quietly since, and his earnings as director are probably no more than $90,000 a year. He keeps a low profile and can walk the streets of his city unrecognized. He can devote time to his wife and two children.

By 1995, Internet and World Wide Web were familiar words.

多都是教育领域的。但不久，电脑使用者了解了这种新型媒体。到2002年，全球大约有六亿人在使用万维网。

毫无疑问，伯纳斯·李拒绝了很多可以挣大钱的机会，挣钱并不是他的目标。他是个理想主义者，追求的是知识。1994年，他加入了马萨诸塞州的电脑科技实验室。从此后，他一直安静地在那里工作。作为主管，他一年的收入恐怕不超过九万美元。他处世很低调，走过大街都没人能认出他。同样他也花很多时间照顾妻子和两个孩子。

到了1995年，因特网和万维网都已成了家喻户晓的名词，这些发明

---

medium *n.* 媒体   idealist *n.* 理想主义者

These inventions made a huge *impact* on modern business and communication. The Web has become a way for many businesses to sell themselves and their products. Companies started to include Web addresses on their business cards and in their advertising. On computer screens today, there are flashing and moving images and advertising of all kinds.

Now, some people think there are things on the Web that are *distasteful*. They want governments to keep this kind of material off of the Web. But Berners-Lee thinks the Web should not be censored. He said, "You don't go down the street, after all, picking up every piece of paper blowing in the breeze. If you find that a search engine gives you garbage, don't use it. If you don't like your paper, don't buy it." (*Technology Review*, 1996 July, pp. 32-40)

Berners-Lee is concerned about security on the Web. He

对现代商业和通讯产生了巨大的影响。万维网已变成许多商家推销自己和自己产品的渠道。许多公司开始将网址写在名片上和他们的广告中。现在，电脑显示屏上，有各种各样闪动的图像和广告。

现在有人认为网上的一些东西很令人反感，他们希望政府能将这些东西删除掉。但蒂姆·伯纳斯·李认为网络不应该被审查。他说，"毕竟你不会走在大街上把每一片风吹的纸片都拾起来，如果发现搜索引擎给你一堆垃圾，你就不去用它好了。如果你不喜欢那些纸，你就不买好了。"（《科技评论》，1996.7，第32页-40页）

伯纳斯·李对网络安全问题非常关心，他建议在屏幕上设一个图标

---

impact *n.* 影响；效果　　　　　　　distasteful *adj.* 令人反感的

suggests having an on-screen *icon* called, "Oh, Yeah?" that can be used by someone who is unsure about something they see on the Web. For example, if someone was shopping online and wanted to make sure that they could trust the company, he or she could click on the icon to receive confirmation that it was safe.

Berners-Lee has received numerous awards for his work on the Web, including a knighthood in 2003 by Queen Elizabeth II for services to the global development of the Internet. This now makes him "Sir Timothy Berners-Lee." Berners-Lee has fought hard to keep the World Wide Web open with no *ownership*, so it is free for all of us to use. We do not know how Berners-Lee will shape the future of the Web. He hopes the Web will become a tool for social change and wants to be a part of that development. The World Wide Web has already revolutionized the way the world learns; now Berners-Lee hopes it can make the world a better place to live.

"Oh, Yeah?", 如果不敢肯定在网上看到的东西是什么, 就可使用这个图标。比如, 如果有人在网上购物, 想知道他是否应该信任这家公司, 就可以点击这个图标来确认是否安全。

伯纳斯·李因为万维网获得了无数殊荣, 包括伊丽莎白二世在2003年因他为全球因特网的发展做出贡献而授予他的爵士封号, 他成为"狄莫西爵士"。伯纳斯·李为使万维网不被某个人所拥有从而向全世界免费开放进行了艰苦卓绝的斗争。我们不知道将来他会怎样规划万维网, 但我们知道他希望万维网能成为有利于社会变革的工具, 成为社会发展的一部分。万维网已经改变了全世界人们学习的方式, 现在他希望万维网能让我们所生活的世界变得更加美好。

---

icon *n.* 图标   ownership *n.* 所有权

A Matter of Laugh and Death

"That joke was really funny; I laughed so hard I almost died!" We've all said this, but of course we don't really mean it.

Try telling that to Alex Mitchell of England. In 1975, he was watching his favorite *comedy* show on television. On the screen, a Scotsman in a *kilt* was fighting a sausage that was trying to kill him. The Scotsman lived, but Mitchell laughed so hard that he had a heart attack and

---

人会笑死吗?

那个笑话好好笑喔，我快笑死了！我们都说过这样的话，但当然我们并不是说真的。

试着告诉住在英格兰的艾力克斯・米契尔吧。在1975年，当时他正在看最喜欢的电视喜剧节目。屏幕上有名穿着苏格兰裙的苏格兰男子和一根企图杀害他的香肠打斗。那名苏格兰男子活了下来，可是米契尔却因为笑得太用力，心脏病发而死。

---

comedy *n.* 喜剧

kilt *n.* 苏格兰式短裙

died.

A few years ago in Thailand, Damnoen Saen-um, fifty-two, started laughing in his sleep. His wife tried to wake him up, but Saen-um kept laughing. Then he suddenly stopped breathing and never woke up again.

If these stories scare you into never laughing again, you might want to *reconsider*. Some studies have shown that laughing is actually good for your health. Regular giggles can reduce stress and even help to fight *infections*. Although laughing too hard can be dangerous, it seems that a laugh a day can keep the doctor away.

几年前在泰国，52岁的丹侬·沙姆在睡梦中开始笑。他的妻子设法叫醒他，但沙姆还是继续笑。然后他突然停止呼吸，再也没有醒来了。

如果这些故事吓得你不敢再笑的话，你也许要重新考虑一下。有些研究显示，笑其实对健康很有帮助呢。常常轻声地笑能减轻压力，甚至有助于抵抗传染病。虽然笑太用力会有危险，不过笑口常开看来可以常保健康呢！

---

reconsider *v.* 重新考虑   infection *n.* 传染病

Brain Power

If someone calls you brainy, it doesn't mean you have a big head. That person is saying you are *intelligent*. Scientists have discovered that the size of a brain is not related to intelligence, though. A human brain weighs about 1.3 kilograms, while a whale's brain weighs in at about nine kilograms. That doesn't mean a whale is smarter than a human.

脑袋灵不灵?

要是有人用brainy来形容你，他并不是指你的头很大，而是指你很聪明，不过科学家发现，脑部大小与智商高低无关。人脑约为1.3公斤，而鲸鱼脑量起来约九公斤，但这并不表示鲸鱼比人类聪明。

intelligent *adj.* 聪明的

The brain also has the longest-living cells in the body. These cells use more than 20% of your body's oxygen' to keep the brain going at top speed. How fast does the brain work? Well, it sends signals at a speed of around 320 kilometers per hour.

To keep your brain in top shape, watch what you eat. Special fats found in fish will give your brain what it needs to perform its best. In addition, certain *vitamins* in eggs improve memory and reaction time. Above all, wear a *helmet* when you're on a motorcycle or playing dangerous sports. By eating right and playing safely, you can be sure your brain will stay in working order.

　　脑部也有人体内活得最久的细胞。这些细胞会消耗人体内超过百分之二十的含氧量，让脑袋保持最佳的活动状态。头脑动得有多快？告诉你，头脑可是以大约时速三百二十公里的速度在传递信号呢。

　　想要有健康的头脑，就得注重饮食。鱼类特有的脂肪，能提供必需的营养，使头脑处于巅峰状态。此外，蛋里有些维生素，能让人记忆力更好、反应更快。更重要的是，骑摩托车或是从事高危险的运动时，一定要戴安全帽。摄取正确饮食、行事小心，就能确保脑袋运作正常。

---

vitamin *n.* 维生素　　　　　　　　　helmet *n.* 头盔

23

Are You Thick-Skinned

My mother says that I'm thick-skinned. This means that if someone says something *critical* about me, I don't get upset. I know my body's skin is not actually thicker than other people's, but just how thick is it?

A person's skin is about two *millimeter* thick, but there are areas on the body that are thicker or thinner. The bottoms of your feet can be as thick as 4.7 mm, while the delicate skin around the eyes

---

你的脸皮有多厚？

我妈妈说我的脸皮很厚。这表示当别人批评我时，我不会难过。我知道我的皮肤并没有真的比别人的厚，但它到底有多厚呢？

人的皮肤大约两毫米厚，但身上有些部分的皮肤会较厚或较薄。脚底的皮肤可以厚至4.7毫米，但眼睛周围细致的皮肤大约只有0.12毫米。这数

---

critical *adj.* 批评的   millimeter *n.* 毫米

is only about 0.12 mm. This may not seem like a lot, but skin is the largest organ of the body.

Although skin is thin, it can stretch and is actually pretty tough. It has to be because it is our first protection against *germs*. With constant exposure to the elements, skin *cells* have to replace themselves quickly. Around 35,000, skin cells naturally fall off every minute, and that's just from one person. You might not want to know this, but , 70% of the dust in your house is made up of shed human skin!

Thick or thin, your skin works hard to protect you. If you take care of it, your skin will continue to take care of you.

字看起来也许不大，不过皮肤是身体最大的器官。

虽然皮肤很薄，但它能伸展，实际上也很强韧。皮肤之所以如此是因为它是我们抵抗细菌的第一道防线。皮肤细胞在持续暴露于外界后必须迅速地更新。每分钟约有三万五千个皮肤细胞会自然脱落，而那只是从一个人身上而已喔！你也许不想知道这件事，但你家里70%的灰尘都是由脱落的人体皮肤组成的。

无论是厚还是薄，皮肤都会善尽职守地保护着你。如果你好好照顾皮肤，皮肤也会继续好好照顾你。

---

germ *n.* 细菌

cell *n.* 细胞

Can You Lift an Elephant **W**ith Your Hair?

Remember when you were a kid and your siblings or classmates got angry at you? If they were like most children, they *yanked* a big handful of your hair—ouch! It may have hurt, but you didn't have to worry about your hair breaking. That's not very easy.

Hair is actually as strong as *steel*. The average head has between

---

头发吊得起大象吗?

你还记不记得，小时候你的兄弟姐妹或同学会对你发飙？如果他们跟多数的孩子一样的话，他们会一把抓住你的头发——好痛啊！头发被扯也许很痛，不过你不用担心头发会被扯断，要扯断头发可不容易呢。

其实头发跟钢铁一样强韧。一般人的发量约为十万到十五万根，这些

---

yank *v.* 猛拉

steel *n.* 钢铁

100,000 and 150,000 strands of hair. Together, all of these strands could lift up to fifteen tons. That's heavier than two African elephants!

Well, you definitely weigh less than two elephants. If your classmates were very strong, they should have been able to pick you up and swing you around by your hair, right? Not quite.

Hair's weakness isn't in the hair itself. Its weakest point is at the *scalp*. If you were to pull someone's hair hard enough, it wouldn't break. It would just pop right out of the scalp. Now that's a *frightening* thought!

头发加起来，能够悬吊的重量可达十五吨，这比两头非洲象还重呢！

你的体重当然没有两头大象重。如果你的同学非常强壮的话，他们应该可以抓住你的头发，把你甩来甩去，对吧？这倒也不尽然。

头发本身并不脆弱，最脆弱的地方是在头皮。如果你用力拉扯别人的头发，头发是不会断的，你只会把头发从头皮直接扯下来，不过这种场面想起来真恐怖！

---

scalp *n.* 头皮   frightening *adj.* 使恐惧的

Where Did the Bones Go?

If you saw pictures of my brother as a baby, you'd be *impressed*. It's not that he was especially cute; it's that he grew from forty centimeters to over 18 centimeters. What you may not know, though, is he has fewer bones in his big body than he did in his baby body.

婴儿和成人谁骨头多?

要是你看过我弟弟小时候的照片，你肯定会感到印象深刻。倒不是因为他特别可爱，而是因为他居然从四十公分长到一百八十几公分。但是你可能不知道，他长大后身上的骨头比婴儿时期的少。

impressed *adj.* 印象深刻的

My brother is not special in having fewer bones now. Almost all *newborns* have about 300 bones. As adults, we end up with about 206 bones, as long as we don't break a leg into pieces on a ski trip.

As babies get older, some of the separate bones grow together to become a single, larger bone. A baby's *skull* is made up of five separate pieces. These pieces get larger, and by the time we reach our teens, their edges have fused into one *solid* bone. If the skull started out in one piece, there wouldn't be enough room for our growing brain!

Even though he has fewer bones than he used to, my baby brother now towers over me. I think some bones just don't want to stop growing!

我弟弟骨头变少这件事并非特例。多数新生儿约有三百根骨头。只要我们没在滑雪时把骨头跌碎，成年后，我们身上的骨头会剩下约两百零六根。

宝宝成长时，有些骨头会合二为一，长成一块较大的骨头。宝宝的头骨有五片，会逐渐长大，等到我们成为青少年时，这五片头骨的边缘已接合起来，形成一整块坚固的头骨。要是头骨一开始就是一整片的话，可就容不下我们日渐长大的脑子！

即使弟弟现在的骨头比以前的少，但是他可比我高得多，看来有些骨头会长个不停呢！

---

newborn *n.* 新生儿
solid *adj.* 坚固的

skull *n.* 头骨

Why Does the Bathroom Smell So Bad?

Maybe there should be a "Danger" sign on the door of the bathroom. The strange sounds and smells that come out of our body in there are alarming. It would be a lot more pleasant if our poo smelled like roses!

The bad smell from poo is mainly caused by *bacteria*. We have hundreds of different kinds of bacteria

---

有没有"香香"的大便？

厕所门口也许该挂个"危险"的标志。我们在上厕所时，身体所发出来的怪声音和气味简直令人惊恐。要是我们的便便闻起来像玫瑰一样香就好啰！

便便的臭味主要是由细菌造成的。我们的肠子里住着上百种不同的

---

bacteria *n.* 细菌

living in our *intestines*. When these bacteria break down the food we eat, they make smelly chemicals and gases.

Not everyone's poo smells the same. Some foods cause more smelly chemicals and smellier poo than other foods. Eating meat, eggs, *garlic*, or *onions* will make your poo smell worse. A horse's or deer's poo doesn't smell as bad because they only eat plants. They also don't add garlic to their meals.

Even if you become a vegetarian, your poo will never smell like flowers. The best thing you can do is to keep a can of air freshener in the bathroom, just in case.

细菌，这些细菌将我们吃的食物分解时，会制造出有臭味的化学物质和气体。

不是每个人的便便闻起来都一样。有些食物会制造出比其他食物更多的恶臭化学物质，也就导致更臭的便便。吃肉、蛋、大蒜或洋葱会让你的便便更难闻。马或鹿的便便闻起来没那么臭，因为它们只吃植物。它们也不会在饮食中加入大蒜。

就算你改吃素，你的便便还是不可能像花一样香。你所能做得最好措施就是放一罐空气芳香剂在厕所里，以防万一。

---

intestine *n.* 肠子   garlic *n.* 大蒜
onion *n.* 洋葱

27

What Would Happen If a Venomous Snake Bit Itself?

They are cold-blooded, hiss, and most people are scared of them. They are snakes.

While most snakes are harmless, about a quarter are *venomous*, and ten percent can kill. The Arizona desert is famous for *rattlesnakes*, and Australia is crawling with death adders. One bite from these and other venomous snakes

---

毒蛇咬到自己会中毒吗？

它们是冷血动物，会嘶嘶作响，大部分的人都怕它们，这种动物就是蛇。

大部分的蛇是无害的，不过约有四分之一的品种有毒，有十分之一足以致命。亚利桑那沙漠以响尾蛇闻名，澳洲则有南棘蛇横行。要是被这些蛇或其他毒蛇咬一口，你可就麻烦大了！但是别担心，蛇只有在害怕的时

---

venomous *adj.* 有毒的   rattlesnake *n.* 响尾蛇

and you're in big trouble! Don't worry, though. Snakes only bite people when they are scared. If you leave them alone, they will leave you alone.

While it's true that venomous snakes can kill people and animals, what would happen if a snake bit itself? Perhaps it strikes at its *prey* but hits its own body, or goes into a frenzy due to panic or extreme cold. Well, the answer to that question is easy—probably nothing. That's because snakes have a special chemical in their blood that stops the venom from affecting them. However, if an African Gaboon viper bit itself, it would probably die. It wouldn't be from the *venom*, but because its teeth are so big!

候才会咬人，所以只要你不去惹它们，它们就不会攻击你。

毒蛇可以杀死人类或动物，那如果它对猎物发动攻击时误伤了自己，或者因为惊慌或极端寒冷而激动自残、咬到自己，会发生什么事呢？这个问题的答案很简单：多半不会有事，因为蛇的血液中有一种特别的化学物质，让毒液对它们不会产生作用。不过如果非洲加彭蝮蛇咬到自己，可能就会死。这倒不是因为毒液，而是因为它的牙齿太大了！

---

prey *n.* 捕食   venom *n.* 毒液

28

How High Can a Bug Fly?

You are driving down the highway and a million insects are hitting your *windshield*. This is pretty common, but have you ever wondered if the same thing happens to airplanes? The answer is yes.

Insects can fly at any height as long as the *temperature* isn't below ten degrees Celsius. On a hot day, that means they can fly as high as 6,000 feet!

昆虫能飞多高?

你行驶在公路上,数以百万的昆虫撞上你的挡风玻璃。这是很常见的现象,但是你有想过相同的情况会发生在飞机上吗?答案是会的。

只要气温不低于10摄氏度,昆虫可以在任何高度中飞行。这表示在天气炎热的时候,它们可以飞到6,000英尺高!

---

windshield *n.* 挡风玻璃   temperature *n.* 温度

Although insects can be thousands of feet in the air, they are not always flying. At that height, they often get carried along by the wind. If the wind carries them into air that's too cold, they freeze. When they drop down to warmer air, they thaw and come back to life.

If you live in a high-rise apartment, this might have you worried. What is to stop a *mosquito* from flying up to your floor to bite you? The answer is experience. Mosquitoes have learned that the bodies (and the blood that's in them) are most *commonly* found on the ground. So don't worry. While the little biters can fly up tall buildings, they probably won't.

虽然昆虫可以到数千英尺的高空中，但它们可不一定是用飞的。在那种高度时，它们通常是被风吹着跑。如果风把它们带到太冷的空气中，它们就会结冻。但是等它们掉到较温暖的空气中，就会解冻而重生。

如果你住在高台大厦，你可能会因此而担心。要怎么让蚊子不飞到你的楼层叮你呢？答案是靠经验。蚊子学到的是在地面上最容易遇见人（及其体内的血液）的本领。所以不用担心，虽然这些叮人的小虫可以飞到高楼上，但它们通常都不会这样做。

---

mosquito *n.* 蚊子　　　　　　　　　　commonly *adv.* 通常地

Do Fish Get Struck by Lightning?

Everyone knows that lightning can kill people. We also know that electricity can move easily through water. So what happens when lightning strikes a lake? Does it cook all of the fish?

Lightning is very powerful and hot. An average bolt of lightning can carry 2 million *volts* of electricity and can create temperatures of 3, 000℃.

鱼会被闪电劈死吗?

大家都知道,被闪电劈到会要人命。我们也知道水容易导电,那么当闪电击中湖面时,会发生什么事?闪电会把湖里的鱼都煮熟吗?

闪电威力强大,会产生高温。平均一道闪电带有两亿伏特的电压,并产生摄氏三千度的高温。

volt *n.* 伏特

When lightning strikes water, however, it behaves very differently than it does elsewhere. On land, all of the energy is *focused* in one place. That is why lightning can kill people and burn trees and houses. When lightning hits water, the energy spreads out in all directions at once. The energy also stays mostly on the surface. The lightning quickly weakens because the energy is *absorbed* by all of the water in the lake.

No one has been able to see exactly what happens to fish when lightning strikes a lake. If fish are swimming close to the surface and the site of the lightning strike, they may be electrocuted. Even so, experts agree that this would be rare. That means for a fish dinner, you'll just have to catch and cook your fish the old-fashioned way.

　　然而，闪电打中水面时的反应和打中其他地方时不同。在陆地上，闪电能量全集中在一个地方，所以闪电能劈死人，通常能造成树木与房屋着火。闪电击中水面时，能量会在瞬间往四面八方散开。闪电能量又大多留在水面。闪电威力会迅速减弱，因为能量已被整座湖水吸收。

　　至今没人能亲眼看见当闪电击中湖面时，鱼儿究竟会发生什么事？如果闪电击中湖面时，鱼群在附近游动，它们也许会被电死。即便如此，专家一致认为这种情况很少见。也就是说，如果你晚餐想吃顿鲜鱼，你还是得用老方法——亲自抓来煮。

---

focus *v.* 集中　　　　　　　　　　　　　absorb *v.* 吸收

30

Do Animals Cry?

We sometimes say that someone is crying "crocodile tears." This means that the person is not sad, but is pretending to be upset to trick you. This saying makes you wonder, though: Do animals cry?

Well, we know that animals show some types of *emotions*. Has your dog ever joyfully jumped around, trying to *lick* your face when you return home? Of course it has. That's what dogs do! Cats

---

动物会哭吗?

我们有时候会说某人是"猫哭耗子"。这是指那个人并不难过,只是假装伤心来欺骗你。不过这句俗语会让你想知道: 动物会哭吗?

我们知道动物会展现某些情绪。你的狗有没有在你回家时快乐地跳来跳去,试着舔你的脸呢? 当然有!这就是狗会做的事。猫儿跌下电视时会

---

emotion *n.* 情感

lick *v.* 舔

can act embarrassed when they fall off the TV, and dogs can feel *ashamed* when you catch them chewing on the sofa. Do they tear up when they lose their favorite toy, though?

Scientists say no. We know that land animals' eyes are wet with tears like our own. These tears kesp the eyes clean and *moist*. The number of an animal's tears does not increase because of an animal's emotions, though. Only humans can do that.

So the next time you're feeling sad, feel special about letting those tears flow.

表现出感到尴尬的样子，而狗在你抓到它们偷咬沙发时会觉得羞愧。可是当它们心爱的玩具不见时，它们会泪眼汪汪吗？

科学家说不会。我们知道陆地动物的眼睛都像我们一样因为眼泪而潮湿。这些泪水能保持眼睛清洁且湿润。不过动物泪水的量并不会因为情绪影响而增加，只有人类会那样。

所以下次你感到难过的时候，应该觉得自己是特别的，让泪水奔流吧。

---

ashamed *adj.* 羞愧的　　　　　　　　　　　　　　　moist *adj.* 湿润的

31

Do Animals Leave Fingerprints?

If a monkey broke into your house and stole a banana, could you use *fingerprints* to track that monkey down and get your banana back? You could, but if your banana was stolen by a kangaroo, you would be out of luck.

This situation may be *ridiculous*, but it presents an interesting question: Do animals leave fingerprints?

动物会留下指纹吗？

如果有一只猴子闯入你家偷了根香蕉，你能凭指纹找到那只猴子拿回香蕉吗？可以喔！但是如果你的香蕉是袋鼠偷走的，那就没这么好运了。

上述的情形也许荒唐，却也提出了个有趣的问题：动物会留下指纹吗？人类手指头上有微小的隆起部位，可以帮我们做一些灵巧的动作。其

---

fingerprint *n.* 指纹　　　　　　　　　　ridiculous *adj.* 荒唐可笑的

Humans have small ridges on their fingers to help them perform delicate movements. In fact, all primates have these ridges, so humans, monkeys, and apes can leave fingerprints. Some monkeys even have "fingerprints" on their tails!

Most other animals do not use their hands or *paws* as much as primates, so they do not have ridges. That's why you'll never catch the kangaroo that stole your banana.

While most animals do not leave fingerprints, striped or spotted animals such as zebras and leopards do have individual *fur* patterns that can be used to tell each animal apart. This isn't exactly the same as fingerprints, but it is useful if you are a scientist, or if you ever have to tell the police which tiger ate your friend.

实所有的灵长类都有这个构造，所以人类、猴子和猩猩都能留下指纹。有些猴子甚至还有"尾纹"呢！

其他动物多半不像灵长类那么常使用他们的手掌或爪子，所以他们没有指纹。这就是为何你永远抓不到偷你香蕉的袋鼠。

多数动物不会留下指纹，不过身上有斑纹的动物，如斑马或美洲豹，它们毛皮上都有独特的花纹，能用来区别身份。斑纹和指纹不尽相同，但如果你是科学家，或者你必须向警方指认是哪只老虎吃了你的朋友，斑纹就派得上用场了。

---

paw *n.* 爪子　　　　　　　　　　　　　　　　　fur *n.* 毛皮

The Thirsty Fish

Do fish get thirsty? The answer seems *obvious*: No. After all, they can drink as much water as they want. A more interesting question is this: Do fish need to drink water? The answer to this depends on the fish.

Fish that live in *freshwater* never drink. Because they have a higher percentage of salt in their bodies, freshwater tends to flow into their bodies naturally.

鱼会口渴吗？

鱼会口渴吗？答案似乎很明显：不会。毕竟它们想喝多少水都没问题。比较有趣的问题是：它们需要喝水吗？这个问题的答案要取决于鱼的种类。

生活在淡水中的鱼从来不喝水。因为它们体内的盐分比例较高，淡水通常自然会流进它们的身体里。

---

obvious *adj.* 明显的   freshwater *n.* 淡水

Many kinds of ocean fish, like tuna and herring, have to drink water all the time for the same reasons humans do. If you have ever drunk *seawater*, though, you might wonder how fish do it. With all that salt, seawater actually makes people thirsty. To handle this problem, fish have special cells in their *gills* that get rid of the extra salt. Without these cells, they could not drink seawater and would die of thirst.

Sharks, however, don't need to drink water at all. They have a special chemical in their bodies that prevents the water inside them from getting out. Because of this, they never get thirsty. Unfortunately for tuna, sharks do get hungry.

许多种海水鱼，像是鲔鱼和鲱鱼，必须不断喝水，理由就和人类一样。但是如果你喝过海水，可能就会想知道鱼儿怎么能喝得下去。因为海水的盐分太多，事实上会使人口渴。为了处理这个问题，海水鱼的鳃里有特别的细胞来排除过量盐分。如果没有这些细胞，它们就不能喝海水而会渴死。

不过鲨鱼完全不需要喝水。它们体内有一种特别的化学物质，可以防止体内的水分流失。因此，它们从不会口渴。不过对鲔鱼来说有一点很不幸：鲨鱼还是会肚子饿！

---

seawater *n.* 海水   gill *n.* 鳃

33

Bloody Steaks?

You have probably seen a rare steak before. It often has a lot of red *liquid* around it, especially if you cut it. What is that red liquid? Is it blood? If you ask most people about rare steaks, they will probably say, "Yes, of course it's blood!" After all, it's red and it's coming from the meat. What else could it be?

牛排里有血吗?

你或许曾看过三分熟的牛排。三分熟的牛排上常有很多红色汁液,特别是在你切肉的时候。这种红色汁液是什么? 是血吗? 如果你问多数人,他们八成说:"当然是血啊!"毕竟这种汁液是红色的,还从肉里流出来,不是血是什么?

---

liquid *n.* 液体

Actually, the liquid is not blood at all. Beef is hung for many days before it is sold so that all the blood *drains* out. The red liquid comes from the cells in the meat expanding and bursting when you cook it. Cooking the steak also causes the fat to break down and mix with the meat, making a red liquid.

So you're out of luck if you want a bloody steak. That doesn't mean that there are no foods with blood in them. Black pudding from England, pig blood soup from Taiwan, and blood stew from the Philippines are all foods with actual blood in them. The only way you'll get a bloody *steak*, though, is if you accidentally cut yourself with the steak knife.

事实上，这些汁液并不是血。牛肉在贩卖前，会晾上好几天，让血流光。肉类在烹煮时，细胞扩张胀破，因而产生红色汁液。烹煮牛排也会让油脂分解，油脂和肉混合，就产生红色汁液。

所以你应该没口福吃到血淋淋的牛排了。但这不代表没有含血的食物。英国的猪血肠、中国台湾的猪血汤与菲律宾的猪血炖，都是带血的食物。只是若想吃到血淋淋的牛排，唯一的可能性，就是切牛排时不小心被牛排刀切到自己。

---

drain *v.* 使流出　　　　　steak *n.* 牛排

34

Why Do Early Birds Sing?

Birds love to sing for two reasons: to attract *mates* and *defend* their nests. Curiously, they sing the most at dawn. Why is that?

Scientists are not completely sure. However, they do have some ideas. First, it is much easier to hear a bird's song in the morning. By lunchtime, the wind and other animals make the world too noisy. If birds want to be heard, they have to start singing early.

为什么早起的鸟儿爱唱歌?

鸟类喜欢歌唱的理由有二,一是为了吸引伴侣,二是为了保卫鸟巢。奇怪的是,它们最常在破晓时歌唱,这是为什么呢?

科学家们还不能完全确定,不过他们是有几个想法。首先,在早晨比较容易听到鸟类的歌声。等到午餐时间时,风声和其他动物的声音会让世界变得太嘈杂。如果鸟类想让自己的歌声被大家听见,就必须趁早开始歌唱。

---

mate *n.* 配偶

defend *v.* 保卫

Second, birds have little else to do during the early morning. The low light makes it hard for them to catch insects, so they sing instead.

Interestingly, birds with bigger eyes start singing earlier in the morning. This may be because their bigger eyes allow them to see possible *predators* earlier (with less light) than other birds can. They know their singing helps predators find them and only dare to begin when they can see.

Next time you hear a bird singing, remember there is a lot more than just *notes* in that song.

第二，鸟类在清晨并没有什么其他的事好做。昏暗的光线让它们难以补抓昆虫，所以它们就转而歌唱。

有趣的是，眼睛较大的鸟类比较早开始歌唱。这可能是因为它们的大眼睛让它们在较暗的光线下能比其他鸟类更早看到可能的掠食者。它们知道歌唱有助掠食者找到自己的行踪，所以只有在看得清楚的时候才敢开始唱。

所以下次你听见鸟类歌唱时，记住，它们的歌曲可不只是音符而已。

---

predator *n.* 捕食者　　　　　　　　　　　　　　　note *n.* 音符

What Makes Rain Clouds Look Dark?

Almost everyone loves looking at clouds on a nice day. You can see all kinds of shapes and *images* in them. One cloud looks like a *bunny* while another may look like a cotton monster. It isn't as much fun to do this on a rainy day, though. For one thing, you will get wet!

Why do the puffy white clouds on a

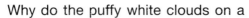

为什么雨天的云是黑的?

多数人都爱在晴朗的日子里抬头看云。你可以看到各种形状和图案的云，有的看起来像兔子，而有的也许看起来像棉花做成的怪物。在雨天看云就不这么有趣了，原因之一是，你会淋湿喔！

为什么蓬松的云在晴天是白色，在雨天却会变黑？答案很简单，云是

---

image *n.* 图像   bunny *n.* 兔子

sunny day turn so dark on a rainy day? The answer is pretty simple. Clouds are made of tiny water or ice droplets. Water is clear, but it scatters and reflects sunlight. That makes clouds appear white.

As a cloud gets thicker with more and more raindrops, the light is *scattered* and *blocked* so much that very little sunlight can get through. This makes the cloud look dark. The more water there is in a cloud, the darker it appears.

If you look up and see that the clouds are getting darker, you know that the sky is filling up with water droplets. Maybe you should grab an umbrella before that water decides to drop on your head!

由小水滴或冰晶构成的，水是透明的，但会分散并反射阳光，所以云看起来是白色的。

当雨滴愈来愈多，云愈积愈厚，光线会大量地被分散与阻挡，因此阳光几乎无法穿透，云层看起来就黑黑的。云层的水愈多，看起来就愈黑。

如果你抬头看到云层愈来愈黑，就知道天空中充满了小水滴，也许你该赶快拿把伞，免得变成落汤鸡！

---

scatter *v.* 分散

block *v.* 阻挡

36

Bye-Bye Love?

You meet. You talk all night, every night, and you can't stop thinking about one another. You've never felt better. You're in love!

Then something happens. The feelings change. There are no more sweaty palms, and the butterflies in your stomach are gone. Mysteriously, it seems that the love is gone. What happened?

Scientists are suggesting that the end of love is not a *mystery* at

---

爱情来去匆匆?

你们俩相遇，你们每晚彻夜情话绵绵，而且无时无刻不思念对方。你从未有过如此美妙的感受，你坠入了情网！

但是某件事发生了，情愫改变了。你的手心不再冒汗，脸红心跳的紧张感也消失了。神秘的是，爱情似乎就此消逝。这是怎么回事？

科学家们指出爱情的终止并非难解之谜。根据意大利研究员恩佐·伊

---

mystery *n.* 谜

all. According to Italian researcher Dr. Enzo Emanuele, romantic love is nothing more than a chemical change in the brain.

Emanuele and his team studied fifty-eight people who had fallen in love. They found the people had high levels of chemicals called nerve growth factors (NGF), which cause feelings of extreme happiness and desire. Within a year, NGF levels had returned to normal, and the extreme feelings were gone.

This may sound depressing for people who believe true love lasts forever, but scientists also believe that long-term love, based on *consideration* and *commitment*, produces its own kinds of special feelgood chemicals. These cause much deeper feelings than romantic love and can stay around for many, many years.

曼纽博士的说法，浪漫的爱情只不过是脑中化学物质的变化。

伊曼纽和他的团队针对58名坠入爱河的人做过研究。他们发现这些人体内的神经生长因子（NGF）含量较高，这种物质可引发极度的幸福和渴望感。但是一年之内，神经生长因子的含量会恢复正常，而亢奋的感觉就消失了。

这个消息可能会让相信真爱永不变的人感到沮丧，不过科学家也相信奠基于关心和奉献的长久爱情可以制造出特有的化学物质让人心情好。这些化学物质引发的感情远比浪漫热恋更加深刻，而且可以维持许多年。

---

consideration *n.* 关心   commitment *n.* 奉献；献身

37

Why Do Leaves Fall?

It's lovely to see the leaves change colors in the fall. It's always sad, however, when winter comes and the leaves fall off. Have you ever wondered why this happens?

Leaves make sugar to help the trees grow. For this, the leaves need water, sunlight, and a gas called *carbon dioxide*. They also make a special plant chemical that keeps the leaves green.

为什么秋冬会落叶？

看叶子在秋天变色是件很美的事，然而冬天来临、叶子飘落时总是令人感伤。你有想过这种现象的成因吗？

树叶制造糖分帮助树木成长。为此，树叶需要水、阳光和一种称为二氧化碳的气体。树叶会制造特殊的植物化学成分，让叶子保持绿色。

carbon dioxide 二氧化碳

All summer, the trees move the sugar from the leaves to their *branches*. When fall arrives, however, there isn't enough sunlight or water for the leaves to make the plant chemical and new sugar. Without the chemical, the green disappears from the leaves, and you see only red, orange, yellow, and brown.

The trees use the stored sugar to *survive* the cold winter, so they are careful not to waste any. If they used the sugar to keep the leaves alive, the whole tree would die. They must let the leaves fall. The trees keep only the leaf buds, so they can grow new leaves in the spring.

　　整个夏天，树木都把叶片制造的糖分移到枝干里，但是当秋天来临时，阳光或水分不足，树叶无法制造植物化学成分和新的糖分。缺少这种化学物质，叶子的绿色就会消失，变成你所见到的红色、橙色、黄色和咖啡色。

　　树木利用储存起来的糖分来熬过寒冷的冬天，所以它们小心地不浪费任何糖分。如果树木用糖分来让树叶活下去，那整棵树都会枯死。它们必须让树叶掉落。树木只留下叶芽，等春天来了，就可以长出新叶子了！

---

branch *n.* 枝干　　　　　　　　　　　　　　　　survive *v.* 生存

38

The Science of Cuteness

What do babies, puppies, and koala bears all have in common? They're all *adorable*! Everyone loves things that are cute, but have you ever wondered why? What is it that makes something cute?

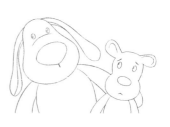

Things that make people say "cute" include round, flat faces, large eyes, and *clumsiness*—all associated with babies. These traits also make babies seem helpless. Scientists agree that this is why we

怎样才可爱?

婴儿、小狗和无尾熊有什么共同点呢?它们都很可爱!每个人都喜欢可爱的事物,可是你有没有想过这是为什么呢?是什么要素让东西变得可爱呢?

让人说"可爱"的事物包括圆圆扁扁的脸孔、大大的眼睛还有笨拙的动作,这些都是和婴儿相关的特征。这些特征也让婴儿看起来很无助。科学家们同意这就是我们喜欢婴儿的原因。我们本能地对无助有所反应,所

adorable *adj.* 可爱的   clumsiness *n.* 笨拙

like babies. We are wired to respond to helplessness, which is also why we want to hold cute things in our arms to keep them safe and maybe squeeze and pet them, too!

As animals get older, they tend to lose the physical signs that make them cute, but animals like pandas and koalas do not. They stay baby-faced and therefore cute.

The *reverse* is true, too. People do not traditionally like wolves or foxes; because their longer faces seem evil or *sly*.

In a day when science and numbers can explain everything, we should not be surprised that science can even explain why things are cute.

以会想把可爱的事物抱在怀里、保护他们的安全。也许会还轻捏或怜爱地摸摸他们！

　　动物长大之后通常会失去可爱的外在特征，但是熊猫或无尾熊这些动物并不会。它们会保持娃娃脸，所以还是很可爱。

　　这点反过来说也是成立的。人们通常不会喜欢狼或狐狸，因为它们长长的脸似乎代表了邪恶或狡猾。

　　在科学和数字能够解释一切的这个时代里，科学可以说明事物为何可爱也不足为奇。

---

reverse *n.* 反面　　　　　　　　　　　　　　　　sly *adj.* 狡猾的

Don't Drop That Coin!

Have you heard the story about a man who was *murdered* by a coin? They say that someone dropped a coin from the top of the Empire State Building. By the time the coin hit a man walking on the street below, it was going so fast that it went right through his head!

Although this story sounds terrifying, it's *simply* not true. As a coin falls, wind and air friction slow it down.

从天而降的硬币会打死人吗？

你有没有听说过有个人被硬币杀害的故事呢？传说有人从帝国大厦顶楼掉了一枚硬币，等到这枚硬币打到街道上的一位行人时，速度已经快到足以穿透他的脑袋了！

虽然这故事听起来很恐怖，但是这根本就不可能。在硬币掉落时，风和空气的摩擦力会使它的速度减缓。最后这会使硬币下坠的速度不再增

---

murder *v.* 谋杀   simply *adv.* 简直

Eventually this causes the coin to stop speeding up. Lucky for us, the fastest speed a falling coin can reach is still too slow to cause damage.

What if someone stands at the top of the Empire State Building and *shoots* a coin out of a gun? Well, the chances of that happening are pretty slim. However, if someone did it, the coin would actually slow down as it fell. Again, it would hurt if it hit someone, but it wouldn't break the skin. For this same reason, normal-sized *hail* doesn't kill people when it falls.

It's still not a good idea to toss anything off of a skyscraper. Use that coin to buy a postcard instead.

加。对我们来说很幸运的是，掉落的硬币所能达到的最高速度还是慢得不足以造成伤害。

如果有人站在帝国大厦顶楼用枪发射一枚硬币呢？这件事发生的机会实在很低。不过，如果真有人这样做，实际上硬币在坠落过程中还是会减慢下来。同样地，这枚硬币打到人会痛，但不至于穿透皮肤。基于相同的理由，正常大小的冰雹掉下来也不会砸死人。

不过把东西从摩天大楼往下丢可不是件好事，还是改用枚这硬币去买张明信片吧！

---

shoot *v.* 发射

hail *n.* 冰雹

How Many Calories Is That?

As anyone who has ever tried to lose weight will tell you, it's all about the *calories*. You can easily find out how many calories food has by reading the nutritional label. What exactly is a calorie, though?

Well, think of the body as a machine. Put simply, you give *fuel* (food) to your machine to make it run. The number of

---

热量有多高?

任何试过减肥的人都会告诉你，减肥的重点在于卡路里。你看营养标示就可以轻松得知食物含有多少卡路里，但到底卡路里是什么呢?

就想象身体是个机器吧。简单地说，你给机器添加燃料，让它运作。卡路里的量告诉我们燃料里有多少能量。

---

calory *n.* 卡路里   fuel *n.* 燃料

calories tells us how much energy is in that fuel.

How do they measure calories? One simple way is by burning the food and measuring how much heat is given off. The process is *complicated* by the fact that our bodies can't actually use all of the calories. To get around this, scientists have found a better way to measure how much our body wastes.

Scientists first get the *recipe*. Then they use chemical tests to figure out how many calories are in each ingredient. By doing this, they don't count the parts of the food that the body won't use.

Now when you see the little calorie number on the food package, appreciate it. A lot of hard work went into it.

那又要如何测置卡路里呢？一个简单的方法就是燃烧食物，然后测量它释放出多少热能。我们的身体实际上并不会用掉全部的卡路里，使得测量程序变得复杂。为了解决这个问题，科学家们发现了一种更好的方法来计算身体会浪费多少卡路里。

科学家们先拿到食谱，然后用化学试验来计算出一样材料含有多少卡路里。这样一来，他们就不会把食物中身体无法吸收的部分算进去。

当你看到食品包装上小小的卡路里数量时，要心存感激。这可是经过许多辛苦的工作而来的喔。

---

complicated *adj.* 复杂的   recipe *n.* 食谱